MIND POWER TO SUCCESS
BY
BILL STILES

Illustrations By:
William S. F. Stiles

DEDICATED TO: Vivian Stiles Ameser, my mother, who used and taught me to succeed with mind power.

ACKNOWLEDGMENTS:

Thank you, **Dick Chaput,** *who taught me to use all that I have,* and thank you, **Bernie Mc-Cardle,** *who showed me the way to thinking beyond the here and now.*

Thank you, **Zig Ziglar,** *for being my example of what we can accomplish by helping others get what they want out of life.*

Thank you, **Robert Scharff,** *for believing in the mind power concept and for patiently working with me.*

A special thanks to my children, **Bill** and **Stacy,** *who helped educate me.*

And finally, loving appreciation to my wife, **Kathy,** *brain trust partner and daily motivator.*

CONTENTS

horses, you gentle them. If we can train
animals, we can train ourselves. How you
can change your life in twenty-one days.

Programming Your Mind 60

Take affirmative action; program your
mind; energize your talents. The magic kit
continued to produce. You are no longer
the same as you were yesterday. The expanded mind never returns to its former
shape. You have the power of a marvelous
mental device. Start your programming
with good imagination. The man who
laughed at a terminal illness. You must
have a strong belief. Don't confuse activity
with accomplishment. Begin a program of
dehypnotizing. Move into the future by
changing whatever causes your problems.
Get rid of bad attitudes by getting rid of bad
behavior. You must change physically. How
to get your forward momentum going. The
danger of backward momentum. Kathryn
Hulme and *The Nun's Story.* How to make
the grass grow greener. A library to program your mind. How to use modern day
technology to accelerate your mind power
program. Make sure you are in action.

Rejoice in Failure 85

It's okay to fail. Some fail at more things
than most people try. Was Thomas Edison
a failure? Never confuse project failure
with life failure. Use "failure time" to reinforce yourself. Look at your original plan.
Analyze what happened. Be a failure problem manager. Maintain your sense of
humor through failure. Establish new plans

to offset failure. Be a cheerleader. Appraise
your competition accurately. Be bold
enough to practice self-love. Some "magnificent" failures.

Habits Run You 99

Liberate yourself from slavery. Ninety-five
percent of your activity is dictated by habit.
Get full control of your mind. You are really
a mind with a body. The difference between you and others is between your
ears. Move into action. Modify your behavior. Make one promise to yourself. Tomorrow is not soon enough. You must coax a
habit down the stairs one step at a time.
Habits indicate what you think of yourself.
Become assertive. Think of your habits as
reactions to situations.

Harness Your Habits 113

Have you ever been pushed around by
someone? You can change and you will.
Fight instead of flight. Aggressive behavior
can become a habit. Reinforce your determination with emotion. Thought control
must start as a conscious effort. Know
what influences your behavior. Learn
about the EAR formula. Change your environment either physically or mentally.
The results of your actions become your
habits. Change your world from bad to
good. Reward yourself.

Use Borrowed Mind Power 123

Review your progress. Develop mental
harmony. Form a brain trust with another

Use the Power of Enthusiasm   **141**

nancial goals. Be health conscious. Serve others. Enthusiasm will enable you to become all you are meant to be.

Practicing Your Mind Power 149

Use your mind power to change opportunity into reality with the mind power trance. How-to exercises that will help you practice mind power. Five goals most people want to achieve. How to achieve the mind power trance. Become more by becoming less. You must convince your subconscious mind by using a daily mind power trance. Now you've got it—go to it!

CHAPTER

1

YOU ARE SOMEONE SPECIAL

You will not be the same tomorrow as you are today. Within the next sixty seconds a change will begin. You will be on your way to having **mind power to success!** Here's why:

Never before has there been another **you**. There isn't another **you**, now. **There never will be another you in all of eternity**. You are special. Accept the fact, the beautiful truth, the marvelous implication of those words and you are on your way! Read them again. Let the meaning saturate your thinking. Now, smile and say to yourself, "That's really so—I am special, a one-of-a-kind person."

Go ahead—do it! Don't read any further until you've tasted and savored the pure, simple, delightful meaning behind the realization that you are a totally unique person. In the sixty seconds it took you to read this far, you have started to use **mind power to success.**

DO YOU WANT TO SUCCEED?

You see, mind power has to do with the fact that you live at the center of your own universe. Nothing is real unless you make it so. Nothing is important unless you deem it to be. Nothing is good or bad, true or false, meaningful or inconsequential, worthwhile or useless, joyous or dreadful until **you** decide that it is. Your universe begins and ends with the way you think about things, not with the way you see them. Your universe and how it's made has nothing to do with what you **see** or with what anybody else **sees.** That's just input. Your universe is what you make of it with your mind. The way you think about things and, further, what you make of them depend on how you put your thinking into action through the application of your **talents** and **abilities.** You've got them! Oh, yes, you have talents and abilities that no one else has because you are one of a kind in all of eternity. You have only to focus those talents and abilities as you would focus the rays of sunshine through a magnifying glass.

Imagine the situation. Suppose you were to focus sunshine through a magnifying glass so that the focal point was held steadily on a piece of paper. What would eventually happen? The paper would catch fire!

FOCUS YOUR TALENTS AND ABILITIES
AND YOU WILL BE "ON FIRE."

Well, you're the same way. Once you decide that you are special and that you have special talents, you can focus those talents and abilities. Then you, too, will be "on fire." You will be ablaze with commitment to directed activities, with important tasks to accomplish and with joyous projects; the world will come to **watch you burn!** What do you think of that? Do you want to discover all that's special in you? Do you want to focus your talents and abilities? Do you want to be on fire with success? Do you want the world to watch? Do you? Do you **really?** Super! Stay with me, because you're on your way.

IT'S EXCITING UP AHEAD

As I write for you I can't put the words down fast enough! I am delighted that you are sharing this message with me. I'm excited about all we have ahead of us to explore. I am pleased to know that what's to come will change your life from now on as you develop your mind power to success. Enjoy with me the excitement of this moment as we quickly review the elements of our upcoming discussions. Know that shortly you will be involved in these concepts that will give you the success you deserve through the use of mind power principles. You have already begun to learn that **you are someone special.** We'll prove that together. This is the first essential for your mind power to success learning.

We'll talk about **why you're afraid.** You are, aren't you? So am I and I always have been. I'm afraid of being criticized. I have always feared poverty—I know what it feels like. I am afraid of losing the love of those I love most. I'm just like you when I fear the finality of death. These fears are always with us, and they stop us from using mind power to success. We'll talk about your fears and discuss ways to overcome them.

I have found that every day presents new opportunities—that in itself doesn't mean anything, though. The opportunities presented to you are as fleeting as a butterfly's hiccup in a whirlwind unless those opportunities are changed into **realities.** We'll discuss how you can recognize opportunities, and I guarantee you'll uncover so many you'll have a hard time selecting those that you want to make real.

After you have selected your most attractive opportunities, the fun will really begin. You'll be amazed to learn how easy it is to enjoy the reality within a few short days of recognizing the opportunity. Just remember: **The real is always better than the imagined.** You'll see!

How you accomplish this will depend, however, on your knowing how your mind works and then making it work. That's a fascinating process. It took me thirty-five years to put the pieces of the puzzle together. You see, this method is not taught in our schools, but we've always had the information at our fingertips. It is presented here in a brief, but clear, form. You will have the pleasure of programming your mind in such a way that achieving goals will seem as if you're on automatic pilot. You'll be amazed at the ease with which you learn new information and make it part of your success program. At this point you'll really be feeling your mind power and, incidentally, **so will all of those around you.** But you're not finished yet; you still have a long way to go.

I failed! Boy did I fail. I still fail and so do you. And you will continue to do so. But don't be discouraged—**you can't fail unless you are doing something.** You're going to be doing more than you ever have, so naturally you're going to have a few things fall through. But, you'll learn how to rejoice in failure because you will be that much closer to success. I can hardly wait to tell you about the things I messed up and how some of them turned around. Stay with me.

Turning failures into victories is a very important part of your mind power to success program. Everything you do has an "up" side and a "down" side. The trouble is, you have been remembering the "down" sides and forgetting the victories of the "up" sides. This has to change. You can do it. You can make victories out of failures.

It will mean changing some of your **habits,** though. Stop and think about it—your habits run you, don't they? Then, it stands to reason that in order to change your life, you'll have to do something about your habits. **Put a harness on them!** Habits will either control you or you will direct them. The biggest stumbling block in your path leading to mind power and success consists of your bad habits. The greatest assistance you will get on your way comes from establishing good and powerful **new** habits. I had to do that. I'll share with you how you can do it.

You'll learn to be patient with yourself and others. It's been said that, "By the yard it's hard; but by the inch, it's a cinch." Of course you can't accomplish **everything** at once. But you can accomplish something each and every day of your life.

That's the beauty of persistently applying the mind power principles. You will be constantly building day after day. It will become so automatic, you will grow geometrically—the more you do, the greater your personal growth and the bigger the reward! You will discover the importance of building step by step. It's just like putting up a house—block by block you build the foundation and board by board you build the frame.

You may ask, "But what about the rest of the world? The people around me? My friends? My family?" We have to consider them and involve them, too. You'll learn about monitoring them as you change and affect their lives. So, bring them along.

You'll learn to **borrow mind power!** Sure you can. It's transferable! Most people go through life and never discover this truth. You can use other people's mind power and, in most cases, they won't even know it. It's a wealth of untapped energy!

Speaking of energy, the **power of enthusiasm** is an unending source that you must plug into and continue to draw from to keep your mind power working. This means you'll have to develop the "stay power" of desire. At this point you'll learn that some of the information in this book can make you unhappy. I regret that, but, once you've read far enough to begin discussing "stay power," it will be too late. Your mind will already be expanded. An expanded mind never returns to its former shape. You will no longer be satisfied with the old you; you'll have to go on.

Then it will be time to put in "sweat equity." Our discussions will be drawing to a close and you'll have your work cut out for you. But know this, you won't be paying a price for success, you'll be enjoying it.

Finally, together, we'll count all the ways you have gained mind power to success and we'll accelerate our program through the use of the **mind power trance system.**

That's what this book is all about. Thanks for inviting me into your mind, for wanting to discover all you can be through mind power. Now, let's talk about why you are so special.

YOUR MAKER THREW AWAY THE PATTERN

You were made to be you and no one else. After you were made, God threw away the pattern. "Thank God!" you may be saying. Oh, yes, I've heard that remark in seminars when I say what I consider to be an obvious fact: We all are different.

"All right," you say. "So be it. What advantage does that give me? Maybe I'd rather not be me." Perhaps you're thinking you would like to have been cast in the mold of Marilyn Monroe, Farrah Fawcett, Albert Einstein, Burt Reynolds, Jimmy Durante...wait a minute. Jimmy "the Schnoz" Durante? you ask. You'll soon see why I've cited him as an example.

All these people in the list are successful. Some are physically glamorous, some are not and most are well known. My point in listing these names is this: Why would you want to be exactly like any of these people? Furthermore, if you aren't using your own talents right now, why do you think you would use the talents of others if you had them? Oops! Pardon me. I didn't mean to step on your toes of self-esteem. But didn't these people use their own talents and abilities to become successful? Their only difference from you is that they found the secrets of focusing their talents. You have talents, too. Success is just a matter of using your talents to achieve your goals.

Take Jimmy Durante. He's my example in anticipation of your thought about wanting the physical beauty of Burt Reynolds or Farrah Fawcett. Jimmy wasn't pretty. He had quite a physical liability to overcome. Many times he was laughed at and turned away. But he conquered this. He focused his talents, he caught fire and the world came to watch him burn!

Next I want to tell you about a woman who decided to commit suicide. She thought she had good reason. All her life, people told her she was unattractive. She couldn't remember ever excelling or doing anything well. She was thirty-nine years old and worked as a scrub woman. Her husband was ill and unemployed. Life for her was one chore after another—no glamour, no pleasures, just drudgery.

Tearfully, she confided in a friend. Her friend asked her to read a book entitled *The Magic of Believing* by Claude Bristol. She read it. The message was temporarily uplifting because it told her that she should believe in herself, figure out what her own special abilities were and focus those abilities, apply them at every opportunity. But, she still wasn't convinced. Like so many people, she thought the message applied to others, but not to her. Her mind was set.

Her friend spoke with her again and asked her to try to remember a time in her life when she was happy and to recall what made her feel that way. She told a story about her high school days when she used to clown around and make her friends laugh. Her friend told her to focus that ability. At last, she did! Today, Phyllis Diller is one of the most famous comediennes in the world.

Dick Chaput may not be as familiar a name as Phyllis Diller, but he is definitely an example of success. When I first met him, he made an impression on me in one hour that truly changed my life. I was living in New Hampshire at the time, trying to be a successful salesman. I was trying to sell toilets, not exactly glamorous products. **Trying** to sell was right. My first year as a toilet salesman was miserable. I tried everything I knew up to that point: calling on plumbers, plumbing wholesalers, hardware stores, just about anyone who installed or distributed the product. Nothing worked. I followed the company training program and used visual aids, but still had little or no success. I knew I was forever going to be a part of the ''selling field of mediocrity.'' I decided to give up and move my family back home to Pennsylvania.

Then one evening, Bernie McCardle, a newly found friend through our church adult Bible class, asked me to go with him to hear a special speaker at the Nashua, New Hampshire, Nazarene Church. He was very insistent.

He told me, ''Bill, this Dick Chaput will show you how to be successful.'' Well, I was all for that. I went, and Dick showed me, indeed. I couldn't take my eyes off him. For about forty-five minutes, Dick talked about a book he had written entitled *All That I Have.* He talked about his philosophy of living. He described his travels and assured us that he intended to increase his speaking engagements in the coming year. Dick managed to accomplish all of this even though he was confined to an iron lung most of the time.

That's right! As an adult, then in his late twenties, Dick had no use of his body from his neck down. From birth he was afflicted with a malfunction which affected his growth, completely paralyzed him early in life and left him with a body only 2-1/2' long. The iron lung helped him to breathe and gave him comfort. The few times that he was removed from his iron lung occurred during his speaking engagements, and it took every breath he had to tell his story.

Dick's story is a simple one. He accepted his condition and **used what he had.** His brain helped him to write books. His sense of

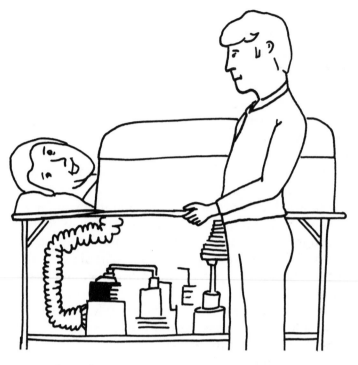

"IT'S ALL THAT I HAVE, AND I'M THANKFUL FOR IT."

humor and keen knowledge of audience reaction enabled him to deliver speeches. Dick totally supports himself in a nursing home in Nashua. As he says, "It's all that I have, and I'm thankful for it."

Dick Chaput is a living example of mind power at work. He was my starting inspiration. I share my experience with you to point out that no matter how cheated you have felt, no matter how little you have, no matter what life has dealt you, no matter where you are today, regardless of burdens or setbacks, you **can** be all that you want to be. In my eyes and in the eyes of thousands of others, Dick Chaput is a person of greatness. And, in my eyes, so are you.

If you and I were to meet face-to-face someday, please know that I would tell you that you are endowed with the same seeds of greatness as the people I have named. When you were made, you were designed to be one-of-a-kind. Your pattern was thrown away, and here you are. You are someone special. The Maker did His job—now it's up to you. What will **you** do with **you** now?

TAKE INVENTORY AND BEGIN WORKING WITH IT

Every man, every woman, every child is his or her own inventory. **You are your own inventory.** You just haven't taken the time to add it all up and put it to its full use to realize the potential that resides within you. Well, it's time to take inventory now.

Take a piece of paper and write down all those things that you do well. This is your **special talents list.** Next, on another sheet of paper, list those activities that were important to you and in which you successfully participated in the past years. This is your **victory list.**

You are doing two very important things:
1. You are isolating your talents and abilities.
2. You are listing successes that you will draw upon to get your mind power working for you.

TAKE INVENTORY AND
BEGIN WORKING WITH IT.

For the next twenty-one days you have an assignment. It's a very pleasant one. Three times a day you are to take your two lists and review them. Don't just read over them and put them away. Look deeply beyond the words. Dwell on the pleasant thoughts. Congratulate yourself. Take an ego trip! Imagine various ways you can use your talents in your neighborhood, at work and at home. Bask in the glory of your past successes as if you were lying in the sunshine. The warm glow you will receive will be every bit as beneficial as the sun's soothing rays. Enjoy. You're having a mental conversation with yourself. You're charging your mind power battery. Keep charging it. I'll tell you how to hook it up very soon.

But first we have to deal with a darker side of you—the fact that **you're afraid, aren't you?**

POINTS TO REMEMBER

1. Believe that you have already begun to change.
2. Know that you are someone special, with talents and abilities that no one else has.
3. Decide right **now** that you want mind power to success.
4. Know that when you focus your talents and abilities, others will immediately notice.
5. Remember that you are endowed with seeds of greatness.
6. Remember Dick Chaput's advice: Use all that you have.
7. Take inventory of yourself and plan to work with it.
8. Make a victory list from your inventory that details your past successes.
9. Be faithful to your twenty-one-day program of charging your mind power battery.

CHAPTER
2
YOU'RE AFRAID,
AREN'T YOU?

There is mind power in courage. There's also mind power in **fear**. Both emotions will drive you; however, they will drive you in opposite directions.

Any change takes courage, and you will feel the fear of taking the first step in a new direction. The bigger the change, the greater your fear. This means that before you can go on, the power of fear must be conquered and replaced with the power of courage.

Look around. Isn't it true that the world is changing every day? Each television news program brings details of the world's shifting circumstances, both the subtle and abrupt changes that influence your life.

Interest rates affect how and where you will live. Petroleum prices erode your disposable income. New laws affecting the core of your existence say what you can and cannot do. Your children are different today from a year ago, and you aren't sure how they will cope with the way things might be when they must find their place in the world. Change—it's happening even now as I share these thoughts with you. It's scary! But here are your choices: **You can either be an agent of the change occurring around you or you can be a victim of it.** Beginning now, the choice is yours! Those who sit and wait, will sit and sit and sit.

All that is changing around you causes anxieties and fears that you constantly feel. Isolate these fears. You will realize as I did some time ago that fears fit into one of five types:

1. **Rejection** by those whose affection you need.
2. **Criticism** of you and your opinions.
3. **Loss** of what you have.
4. **Poverty** and deprivation.
5. **Death.**

I have felt all of these fears, and from time to time I still feel them. Yet, I know that to go forward, fear must be overcome. To do that, it's necessary to conquer that which is feared.

OVERCOME YOUR FIVE BASIC
FEARS AND YOU WILL DEVELOP
THE POWER OF COURAGE.

I KNOW HOW YOU FEEL

The following is a short list of some of the fears I have experienced in my life:

- I feared the town bully when I was a teenager because he insisted he was going to beat the daylights out of me—and he did!
- I feared leaving home and familiar surroundings to explore the world and seek unknown places and different people.
- I feared facing my first customer as a young salesman.
- I feared speaking to a group of twenty salespeople who invited me to share my techniques of successful selling; later, I feared facing a convention audience of two thousand as a banquet speaker.
- I feared investing the equity in my home against the risk of a real estate venture.
- I feared dying as I was rushed to the hospital for emergency surgery to remove a piece of steak that was caught in my throat.
- I feared being thought stupid when I presented untried ideas in a corporate boardroom.
- I feared rejection of my first book by a publisher.
- I feared taking the risk of getting into a new business.
- I feared rejection of my marriage proposal to Kathy, the woman with whom I wanted so much to share the rest of my life.

There are hundreds of other fears that have been part of my ever-changing activities. Please understand that I am not writing about myself because I enjoy reading stories of my life. That would certainly be an exercise in conceit—a disease that makes everyone sick except the person who has it. I'm telling you about my feelings and what I have done with them to let you know that I have walked in your shoes, felt what you feel and faced circumstances similar to those you face every day.

Overcoming your fears is all in the approach—how the fears are met and how the object feared is **conquered.** Each time I conquered a fear I grew and gained additional mind power to propel me to success I did not previously enjoy.

Here's how I conquered the fears I listed earlier:

- Facing the bully got me a whipping, but as he made a "meal" of me, I got a good-size "sandwich" out of him, and he never bothered me again because his bruises hurt as much as mine did. As a result, my self-esteem was greatly increased.

- Leaving home and exploring the world gave me new ideas that showed me how to rise above the field of mediocrity.
- Selling and, therefore, conquering my first customer gave me the confidence to do it again and again until I became a national selling champion.
- Sharing my selling techniques with the group of salespeople led me to become a sales trainer and entirely changed my career direction. Speaking before an audience of two thousand convinced me that I could successfully reach many at one time and led to hundreds of speaking engagements all over the United States, Canada and Mexico.
- Investing my home equity eventually parlayed that rather modest sum into holdings of half a million dollars in real estate in less than two years. Those properties are growing in value every year.
- Fearing for my life showed me how fragile the human body is and how important it is to take care of the physical part of me. This pays dividends every day.
- Presenting ideas in business situations showed me I wasn't stupid. Nobody had come up with the ideas before, and they meant good returns on investment for my employer and, ultimately, for me and my family.
- Daring to write my first book on selling and then finding a publisher for it accelerated everything I was attempting to do as a trainer and consultant.
- Taking advantage of an opportunity to buy a business, a beauty shop, not only resulted in a successful venture, but also was the beginning of a new life with Kathy, whom I met through that business.
- Asking Kathy to marry me has resulted in the happiest years of my life, thus far.

The point of the preceding examples is that each success, small or large, was the result of **change**. First, I felt the fear and admitted I had the feeling; then I conquered the cause of the fear and used the mind power contained in courage to move forward. You should note that in each example overcoming the fear and then moving forward involved **risk**.

RISK A LITTLE TO GAIN A LOT

What do you want out of life? What changes are you to be a part of? What new direction will you take? Where do you want to be in a year from now, five years, ten years or at retirement? When will you take action to move in your new direction? How will you accomplish your goals?

No matter what you attempt to do, you will find that every move will involve risk. Risking will give rise to fears described earlier, and these fears will tend to keep you from the very thing that you want out of life. Because of this you are constantly in danger of maintaining your status quo and falling victim to your own cautious, nonrisk-taking nature while the world changes around you.

Whether you desire a new relationship with another person, a change in jobs, a new business venture, an opportunity for full use of your talents or just a chance to explore, you have to be willing to risk something of what you already have so that you can gain your objective. That does not necessarily mean you will lose or give up anything you have; it just means that you must at least risk it. In most cases you'll find that what you risk is retained, and you will add your desired objective. This is what growth is all about. This is success in every case where you achieve your preestablished goals.

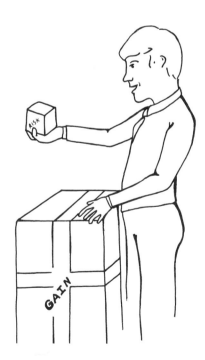

YOU MUST RISK A LITTLE
TO GAIN A LOT.

How do you go about analyzing what must be risked and whether or not the risking is worth the desired result? How do you minimize potential loss in the face of expected gain? How do you use the mind power aspects of courage and control the negative power of fear? Helen Keller once said, "Security is mostly a superstition. It does not exist in nature. Nor do the children of men, as a whole, experience it. Avoiding danger is no safer in the long run than outright exposure. Life is either a daring adventure or nothing." This means that in order to grow you must give up the idea that doing certain things will bring you security. Look at the people who work in the same company for twenty years only to have the company go bankrupt and leave them with nothing. Look at those who dedicate themselves to one mediocre task all of their lives only to find the payoff is a gold watch and a pension that won't cover the cost of living in the rising tide of inflation. Look at all those who say in the winter of their lives, "I had a chance, but I passed it up."

If you are going to do anything with your life, you must overcome your fears and take risks. You must commit yourself to action. When you take risks you will find that you are able to outpace yourself. You will be able to go beyond what you previously saw as being your limits. You will see that as you reach your goals uncertainty and danger are just part of growing.

You have to put your cards on the table to know whether or not you have a winning hand. You have to begin letting go of what you think is certain in order to get what you think might be better than what you have. If you are not willing to risk you will not find love, power, prestige, money, time, happiness or growth.

ARE YOU HONEST WITH YOURSELF?

Are you honest with yourself? Are you clinging to false beliefs that hold you back and keep you from taking risks that would give you the growth you need? For example, do you tell yourself, "I could really do that if I tried," and then let that belief hold you back? This kind of thinking lulls you into a sense of false security that keeps you from **real** growth. Thoughts like that will keep you from accepting a better job or changing from a bad situation to one that is better for you.

Beware of false beliefs; they keep you from taking the little risks that could lead to big gains. You're afraid, aren't you? You fear being tested. You fear the embarrassment of failure. Therefore, you don't try. Instead, you play the mind game of "I could have if I had put my mind to it!" **Could have is not the same as doing.** Many people are so afraid of losing something when they make a change that they avoid all risks. In every case, they settle for something less than they should.

ADMIT YOU'RE AFRAID AND MOVE ON

You have to be very honest with yourself. Admit you are afraid. Admit you fear losing something as you take risks. Stating your fear will be your first step on the road to making a change. It will help you let go of the past and move ahead to a brighter, better future.

When do you begin? Now! The perfect time to move ahead will never come sometime in the future. The time is now. Your success will depend on your taking action, on risking, not so much on your analyzing the fears and potential losses. Don't worry, I would never encourage you to risk all you have for a pie-in-the-sky pipe dream. This can be worse than not risking at all.

PLAN WELL AND PUT YOUR PLAN INTO ACTION

You don't want to be one of those people who gets into one mess after another. You don't have to be. You can make changes, take risks and grow without creating chaos in your life. So, before you take action, you have to know what you want and have a plan to accomplish it.

How do you know that now is the time to take a risk? To move on? Remember, the person you become is the result of your feelings. If you feel unhappy, you will be unhappy. Your first step is to admit that you do not have what you want out of life. You don't feel the way you want to; you are just **not happy!**

Isn't that why you're reading this book? Isn't that why you have read this far? Aren't you hoping to find the answers that will give you mind power to success as promised in Chapter 1? Well, relax; the answers are here. Stay with me for the second step in overcoming your fears and taking the risks that will propel you forward.

Your first step was to admit that you are unhappy. You won't lose anything by doing this except your false beliefs, pretending day after day that you are happy with what you have when you really aren't. If you wait for something to happen on its own to change things for you, you are just programming yourself for failure.

For the second step you must honestly evaluate your risks. Answer these nine questions to decide if each risk you plan is worth taking:

1. Is it necessary for my well-being that I make a change?
2. Is it possible to achieve what I want in another way, thereby minimizing the risk I must take?
3. Could I lose much more than I will gain? (Be careful here. Don't use this as an excuse.)
4. What exactly can I lose by moving ahead?
5. Will there be evidence of the loss?
6. As part of my plan, how can I provide steps that will help me stop these losses so I can eventually **have it all?**
7. How must I improve my knowledge to limit the losses as I go about taking a risk?
8. Who can help me get the knowledge I must have before making a move? What books will help?
9. What other people have been successful doing what I want to do?

When you respond to these questions, write your answers in as much detail as you can. Seek information from other people. Keep expanding your thoughts in every category. You should end up with several paragraphs in response to each of the nine questions. This written material becomes the first draft of your plan of action. Now, ask yourself a tenth question: What is the ideal time to execute my plan? As you answer this question consider this hypothetical situation:

Suppose that there was a bank where, at the beginning of each day, a credit of $86,400 was put into your account. This is an unusual account, however, because no balance will be carried over from day to day. Every evening the remaining unused cash will be canceled. You will be able to use whatever is there for the day, but the unused part will be wasted. If you had such an account, what would you do? Naturally, you would use as much of the money each day as you could.

EVERY MORNING THE BANK OF TIME CREDITS YOUR ACCOUNT WITH 86,400 SECONDS.

Good news! You do have such an account. It's open in your name. This generous bank is **time**. Every morning the **Bank of Time** credits your account with 86,400 seconds. Every night it cancels the amount that you haven't invested in your life toward your growth. If you fail to use today's deposits, you will lose them forever. As Theodore Roosevelt said, "Nine-tenths of wisdom consists of being wise in time." So, the best time for putting your plan into action is **now!**

And about risk, Roosevelt advised us, "Far better it is to dare mighty things, to win glorious triumphs, even though checkered in failure, than to rank with those poor spirits, because they live in the gray twilight that knows not victory nor defeat."

Being afraid is natural and proper. But, admit your fear and deal with it. Dealing with fear and moving on in spite of it gives you the mind power contained in courage that will change your small risks into big gains.

NOW ON TO YOUR SUCCESS OPPORTUNITIES

Conquering that dark or fearful side of you prepares you for the next step as you acquire greater mind power to success. You're all set! You're ready to look at the world around you and discover that opportunities are waiting for you. You're about to discover that recognizing these opportunities is the starting point which will determine the difference between success and failure. You're about to learn that even though opportunity is knocking, you must still get up and open the door.

Are you ready to find your opportunity? Are you eager to get on with it? Okay. Go on to Chapter 3 and see how your **opportunities abound!**

EVEN THOUGH OPPORTUNITY IS KNOCKING, YOU MUST STILL GET UP AND OPEN THE DOOR.

POINTS TO REMEMBER

1. Know that there is power in both **courage** and **fear,** but their power will drive you in opposite directions.
2. Change will cause anxiety, but you must change to move ahead.
3. The world is changing around you, and if you aren't an agent of that change, you'll be a victim of it.
4. Each time you conquer a fear, you will gain additional mind power that will propel you forward.
5. You **must** risk a little to gain a lot.
6. If you maintain your status quo you will not grow.
7. The only security in life is the ability to produce.
8. Be honest with yourself by not clinging to false beliefs that hold you back from true achievement.
9. Admit your fear and move on.
10. Plan well and then put your plan into action.
11. Make good use of your daily time deposit in your Bank of Time account.

CHAPTER

3

OPPORTUNITIES ABOUND

A few moments ago I opened my mail. In it was a contract for a seminar in Cincinnati at a meeting of the Cincinnati Purchasing Managers' Association. I did work for them last year and they want more. I also received a letter from David Kellough, executive director of the North American Heating and Air-Conditioning Wholesalers, inviting me to do four regional seminars. This is a result of a mini-seminar I did for the wholesalers two weeks ago. Also as a result of that seminar, I booked a sales training session in Milwaukee and another in Washington, D.C.

Earlier today I went to see about starting merchandise selling auctions in Lakewood Pavilion, a large building in an old park that I bought a few years ago. The selling auctions will be a new business venture that will start in about three weeks.

My wife Kathy called me from our beauty shop this morning to tell me that this week will be a record-breaker for our business. Opportunities abound!

And not only today. Yesterday I booked a program for the York Air-Conditioning Company at their annual sales meeting in Oklahoma City, and I also agreed to do five articles on selling for *The Wholesaler,* a national trade magazine based in Chicago.

Last month I gave a talk to the St. Regis Paper Company, and now they want another for their entire selling organization. Plus, I had a call to see if I would be interested in selling the coal rights to my forty-two-acre farm. One opportunity after another!

MY SITUATION CAN BE YOURS, TOO

"Stop! Enough!" you must be saying. "That's not me, that's **you!**"
Well, **it can be you, too!** Once you take advantage of opportunities,
they come in an unending flow. I am just like you. I told you I've
walked in your shoes. I know how you feel. I know where you are and
I know where you can go.

The opportunities I described are the results of years of risk taking,
hard work and grabbing every chance at every turn. My success
today is far removed from what my situation was years ago.

I knew poverty as a child. My family lived in a housing project. I had
no shoes to wear to grade school until the Reverend Mr. Mink from
our church gave me some used shoes. Dad was in the hospital and
had no company compensation; Mom had four little children to
watch over. I will never forget the embarrassment of going to school
wearing patched, secondhand clothes and hearing the ridicule of
others. We were called "project kids" and lots of other names.

When I was twelve I scrubbed floors in a local dairy store to help
pay for my family's food. At sixteen I had three jobs in addition to
high school: I worked in a drugstore as a stockboy, in a clothing store
as a window washer and general "go-for" and in a dairy store as a
busboy. Yet, I knew positively, without any doubt, I was destined to
be successful. Even then I had what I now call **mind power to success.** I believed that I, like you, was endowed with the seeds of
greatness and that I was, in my early years, cultivating the ground
that would allow me to plant these seeds of success for a later
harvest. I was sure that even in Ellwood City, Pennsylvania, a
community of 16,000 people, there was opportunity for me.

Without knowing I was using the principles of mind power to
success, I began with a healthy certainty that I was someone
special—even if no one else thought so. I was putting into action a
mind power mechanism that I will be discussing in this chapter. As I
looked to my future I visualized myself as a successful individual.

When I was sixteen, I heard that WKST, a radio station in the
larger neighboring town of New Castle, was going to put a small
remote broadcast station in Ellwood. Opportunity! My imagination
went wild! Suddenly, I saw myself as a radio announcer sitting
behind a microphone with turntables on my right and left. I imagined
my friends from high school listening to me over the radio. What a
magnificent fantasy that was! As I visualized this, it became more

and more real. Finally, it was so real all I had to do was set things in motion that would lead to that very moment.

On opening day of the remote station, I was there. Bob Grant, the announcer, was conducting a "man on the street" interview and I stood next to him. I told him what a wonderful opportunity it was for Ellwood City and its merchants to have their own broadcast station. Bob asked me to explain what I meant and I elaborated. I told him I thought the youth of the community should also be represented and that he should develop a weekly program called "Disc Jockey of the Week." I said that he could invite guest high school students to spin their favorite records. After we went off the air, I offered to host the show each week and bring in guests. I also told him that I would sell spots for the show by getting local merchants' support. Did he buy it? You bet. Suddenly, I was a teenage radio personality in three counties, a small opportunity that I visualized and made into a reality.

How many teenagers do you suppose thought of the remote broadcast station as an opportunity for them? Well, I happened to be the only one who showed up with such an idea that day. Did I give up my other jobs? No, I needed them for money. But eventually, one of the radio station's full-time disc jockeys left. Whom do you suppose got the job? Yes, I did. At sixteen I became the host for a program called "Night Shift" that became popular with the young people in the community. **Then** I gave up my other jobs.

In addition to my radio job, I wanted to expand my exposure as a spokesman for local teenagers. I approached the editor of the *Ellwood City Ledger* and asked if he would be interested in a column that I would title "Teenage Views" and in which I'd write about current events. He was interested. I began a writing career. **More** opportunity just waiting for me. What next?

Opportunities seem to cluster around each other. Once the mechanism for achievement is set in motion, one thing seems to lead naturally to another. Guess who was elected class president, drama club president, yearbook manager and who received more recognition than he ever thought possible? Opportunities abounded for me!

Do you see in these examples what we can learn about opportunities when we're young? Today, I consider the world to be my territory, but when I was a teenager, my territory was Ellwood City. The point is that opportunity exists for you in your own backyard. Wherever you are, it's there for you to grab.

Do I forsake my home base, even now? Of course not. I continue to see opportunity at home while enjoying the opportunities of a career that takes me many miles away. I know that I must still take advantage of things at my doorstep. For example, look at the chain of events involving the old park and dance pavilion that I bought.

One evening I saw an ad in the real estate section of the newspaper for Lakewood, a small old park in New Castle. The package included a huge dance pavilion, two houses, seventeen acres and a dried-up lake. Most people in the community considered the property useless. Still, it caught my imagination. However, all of my money was tied up in my home, which is a forty-two-acre farm. I went to three banks to see if they would lend me the money for the park. All of them refused, which made me even more determined to buy it.

I asked area residents why there was no water in the lake. They told me that many cottages had been built around the water and sewage from them had polluted the lake, making it unfit for swimming. Also, the stream that fed the lake had washed silt down for many years and, consequently, the lake bed was filled with sediment. Armed with this information, I had a core sample taken of the lake bed and was convinced that I wanted the property. I prepared a plan, took pictures of the property and my farm and made a proposal to an out-of-town bank. Using the equity in my farm, I acquired Lakewood. There was no money down, just a matter of risking my home.

You see, there are about 150,000 tons of soil in that lake bed. The soil was washed downstream from fields miles away, which farmers had been fertilizing for years. The whole process produced **super alluvial topsoil** for me! That soil today sells for $3 per ton wholesale, and the price is going up every year. I haven't mined it yet, but someday I will. To everyone else it was junk. To me it's a treasure. When the dirt is sold, the lake will be filled with water and Lakewood once more will be a park for picnics, swimming and boating. We might even put in waterslides. Lakewood became a "pay dirt" opportunity, indeed.

Also, remember the big dance pavilion I got with the purchase? Well, at that time, disco dancing was the rage, so I put in a disco. Lakewood is located in Hickory Township, a "dry" community. That was all right with me, though. I wanted my disco to be for teenagers. For three years, we really packed them in every Friday and Saturday night.

Today, the property is worth eight times the purchase price. Recently, the township put in a million dollar sewer line and all of the cottages around the lake hooked up. So, Lakewood is clean.

WHAT WAS JUNK TO EVERYBODY ELSE WAS A TREASURE TO ME!

I had to **believe** in that venture, didn't I? I had to risk my home. I had to see the opportunity to make a reality out of it.

SEARCHING HIGH AND LOW FOR OPPORTUNITY

Where should you go to find opportunity? Must you pack, leave your hometown and search in the great metropolitan areas of our country? Should you change jobs? Can you stay close to home, family and familiar surroundings?

All of these examples are ways of finding new opportunities that will help you on your way to success. In some cases, a physical move will enable you to take advantage of special opportunities that don't exist in your hometown. However, a physical move is certainly not necessary. In my own career I have moved twelve times. Each move was to seek additional opportunity. Each move helped me to achieve. Every time I moved I believe that I grew. However, I assure you that my greatest growth was accomplished not by moving but by remaining in one place for ten years—isolated on my farm in a serene environment. You can find success right where you are! There are opportunities in your own backyard that you are overlooking **every day!**

In Russell Conwell's famous lecture delivered all over the country during the late 1800s and early 1900s, he told the story, "Acres of Diamonds," which stresses the importance of searching your own backyard for opportunity before you look anywhere else.

The story goes like this: A Persian farmer who lived near the Indus River in India had heard that true wealth could be had by owning diamonds. This farmer was a wealthy landowner, but he became obsessed with the idea of owning diamonds; he wanted to be the wealthiest of the wealthy. Thus he began his search.

So he could devote all of his time to looking for diamonds, he sold his farm and sent his wife and children to live with his brother. Years passed. Finally, all of his money had been squandered. Broke, discouraged and depressed, he committed suicide. One day, some years later, the man who bought his farm was watering his camel at a pond on the property and noticed the sunlight reflecting on a shiny, black stone nestled in the sand at the bottom of the pond. It was a diamond, the first one discovered in what was to become the largest diamond mine of all time—the Golconda! Yes, there were acres of diamonds in the farmer's own backyard. Opportunity had virtually stared him in the face, but he overlooked it.

Then there was the incident around Titusville and Oil City, Pennsylvania, where the first major oil discovery in this country was made. It all began when a young man was discouraged about trying to raise cattle. The water on his farm was polluted with coal oil. He knew what it was. He'd had it tested. He also knew there was a market for this stuff for oil lamps, but he wanted to raise cattle. Disgusted, he sold his farm for $833. Eventually, millions were made on the sale of that oil, but not by the original owner. Another backyard opportunity missed!

VISUALIZE YOUR OBJECTIVES

In the early '70s, a Greek immigrant and his family moved to New Castle, Pennsylvania. He Americanized his name and insisted that everybody call him "Bill." To make a living he opened a little sandwich shop in a small building where three fast-food restaurants had not been able to stay in business. But Bill did something different. He visualized himself as being successful. He saw people coming into his sandwich shop for something special. He didn't quite know what that specialty might be, so he asked as many people as he could what they would like to have in a sandwich. What initially looked like confusion became his offering and ultimately the basis of his success. Bill found out that the people of New Castle wanted something different from the usual burger and fries. He gave them cold cuts, hot dogs, tuna fish and any other concoction that he was asked to put together. Today, a few years after opening his first shop, he owns four sandwich shops and plans to open more. Someday you might see one of his shops in your hometown.

Visualizing your success is a proven method of your mind power at work. It worked for Bill and for another New Castle resident as well.

A young man named Columbus wanted to be successful in business. However, he had little education and believed he had no talents. But, for some reason he had just awakened to the fact that he was a man who wanted to do something with his life. He, too, visualized himself as a success. He saw himself in a fancy office with many employees and a huge bank account. Because of this visualization, he was on his way! He put mind power to work. His success mechanism became activated! Realizing that opportunity is sometimes dressed in work shoes and overalls, he decided to do what he knew how to do best: He was determined to become the best **janitor** in the community.

He formed Columbus Services and worked his brooms, scrub brushes and window cleaning tools day and night. Soon many small merchants and some larger companies heard about his excellent service. New doors to opportunity opened every day. More correctly

COLUMBUS IS SWEEPING UP BECAUSE HE KNEW OPPORTUNITY SOMETIMES COMES DRESSED IN WORK SHOES AND OVERALLS.

stated, **Columbus opened** these doors whenever they appeared! He had so many cleaning and maintenance contracts that he had to hire a crew, then another and another. The money came in and Columbus was suddenly in the position of needing investments to protect his income. He bought the only hotel in town, the Castleton, where he had worked for minimum wage as a janitor. Then he built his own office building and his own warehouse.

Actually, I've lost track of everything Columbus is involved in now. I last heard that he had acquired the cleaning and maintenance contract for the Pittsburgh International Airport. In eight years, he moved from a minimum wage earner to one of the most successful businessmen in New Castle. He visualized the goal. His success mechanism went into action. He used mind power and sweat equity and found opportunity in his own backyard.

What about you? Is there opportunity for you right where you are? Let's see how you can find it.

GET YOUR "GOAL-FINDER" WORKING

Are you oriented toward success? Is your goal-finder working? What do I mean by that? It's simple. Some people are continually tuned into success and perceive opportunity when it is present. Others are not tuned into success and miss every opportunity around them. Your mechanism for finding opportunity works only in an environment of **goals** and **results.** You must give the mechanism that I call a **goal-finder** a definite mission to complete. When that is accomplished and you have a stated objective, your goal-finder will point you to opportunities better than any specific plan you could set forth yourself. All you have to do is supply a goal and keep thinking what the result will be when you reach that goal. Your goal-finder will supply the opportunities along the way to guide you toward your objective. For example, if you must come up with new ideas, your goal-finder will supply them. If you must find someone with a special area of expertise to help you, your goal-finder will search until that person is found.

Read again some of the examples at the beginning of this chapter. You will see that the stories had a happy ending because the individual had visualized the goal as having already been achieved. Every person who met his objective had put his goal-finding mechanism into action. Although this mechanism has always been with us, some of the greatest people have failed to recognize its power.

Thomas Jefferson, as brilliant as he was, missed the impact of the goal-finding mechanism in people. Jefferson thought it would take a thousand years to settle the West. He underestimated what can be accomplished when free men visualize an objective and have a goal. Opportunities presented themselves and our forefathers used every available means to accomplish their task.

You must **see** the result! You must know what you want. Think that your objective is entirely possible and you will activate your

YOU HAVE A GOAL-FINDER. YOU MUST TUNE YOURSELF AND GET YOUR GOAL-FINDER WORKING.

goal-finder. By visualizing the end result your brain begins to see the objective as something that is real **now!** Your entire nervous system, all of your thinking and subsequent behavior relate directly to that objective. In fact, after a very short period of time you will begin feeling as if the objective has already been reached. Opportunities to fulfill your goal will present themselves. Your goal-finder will be working subconsciously day and night to find ways to accomplish your task. It will also reject ways that will keep you from success.

HOW DO YOU FACE THE DAY?

There are two ways for people to face the start of a new day. One way is to say, "Oh, my, another day. I wonder what terrible thing is going to happen to me?" The other way is to get up and say, "Oh, wow, another day! This is what I want to do with it." People who face the day this way are the ones who find opportunity and use it to achieve their goals. How do **you** face the start of the day? How have you faced it up to this point? Do you worry? We all do from time to time, but some worry more than others; it's an ingrained habit. When you worry, you are engaging in the first way of looking at your day; that is, you anticipate the worst for no reason.

Why do I talk about worry now? Basically, worry achieves the opposite of what thinking positively about your goal will. Worry is looking at the future expecting a **negative** result. When you do this you begin to feel the same negative feelings that you would if the troublesome event actually happened. Through worry, you picture yourself as having failed. Can you expect good things to happen when your mind is saturated with the dread of negative results? Will your goal-finder be able to propel you toward success when your thinking moves you in the opposite direction? Of course not.

Your brain and your nervous system can only react to the way you program them. This automatic, built-in mental device cannot tell the difference between real and imagined experiences. All that you feel, both good and bad, becomes a part of your life.

GET READY TO MAKE YOUR OPPORTUNITIES INTO REALITIES

You want to choose thoughts that will start your goal-finder working in the direction that **you** desire. Start now. Program yourself with **good, powerful** thoughts that give you the feeling of having accomplished your goals. Set your mind. Focus your talents and abilities. Throw yourself forward by perceiving the future you want for yourself and activate your goal-finder.

Remember how special you are. Review your victory list. Go over your goals that you established as you made a plan in Chapter 2. Work toward accomplishing these goals. Be persistent. You'll begin finding opportunities immediately and be on your way to changing those opportunities into realities.

POINTS TO REMEMBER

1. There are opportunities everywhere for everyone.
2. There can be acres of diamonds in your own backyard.
3. Realize that you have a built-in functioning goal-finder to help you achieve what you want.
4. To get your goal-finder working you must visualize the result of your plan for success.
5. Get up in the morning expecting good things to happen.
6. Stop the worry habit because it programs your goal-finder with negatives.
7. Your brain and nervous system cannot tell the real from the imagined. What you think, both **good** and **bad,** will become a part of you.
8. Review your victory list and your goals.

CHAPTER

4

CHANGE OPPORTUNITY TO REALITY

It's review time! To keep everything in focus, here's what we've discussed so far:

You are someone special and have a responsibility to yourself to do everything with your talents and abilities that you possibly can. In order to accomplish that mission, it's necessary for you to focus your talents. The more you use them, the more you will have to use!

You had an assignment to see yourself as being successful in whatever you want to do. These imagined mental victories will be very real to your subconscious mind, and you'll begin getting feedback that will help you feel successful and will tend to change your imagined successes into real ones. You want that! Remember, the real is always better than the imagined.

You were supposed to make a victory list and go over it every day. If you have put it off—stop! Don't read any further because you're not ready. Go back, make up your victory list and get into the program.

Then, we discussed your being afraid. You realize that any change brings about some feelings of uncertainty. Anxiety is natural because you're afraid you're going to lose something in order to gain. You know, though, that security does not exist in nature. The only security we have exists between our ears; that is, in our minds and how we think. That thought process dictates our ability to produce. This individual personal production leads to what we call security.

Finally, remember that there is an abundance of opportunity all around you. Set your goals. Decide on targets. Think about your objectives, and opportunities will present themselves to help you accomplish them.

Is that all there is to it? Well, some people who subscribe to the self-help program of maintaining a positive mental attitude would advise you that it is at least 90 percent of the battle. Most would say that good things will continue to happen and that one good thing will lead to another. Sorry, it just doesn't work that way.

MY GOAL-FINDER MUST BE BROKEN

You see, I had always believed that one thing would lead to another. As I set my objectives and visualized myself successfully achieving them, my goal-finder seemed to kick right into high gear. Then, thud! Something happened, everything was going wrong. All of a sudden I couldn't get where I wanted to go. I couldn't achieve. I was failing. I stopped making progress. Opportunities still presented themselves, but I couldn't take advantage of them. I continued to set goals, bigger and bigger ones, but I couldn't accomplish them. People and circumstances began to get in the way of what I wanted to do. Time after time I failed. Was my goal-finder broken?

I THOUGHT MY GOAL-FINDER
WAS BROKEN.

I thought perhaps my goals were too unrealistic, that I was shooting for targets impossible to hit. But how could I lower my goals when there were still many opportunities that begged to be turned into realities? And I knew that somehow, some way I **could** have the reality of greater accomplishment. But there was the rub. Could you see it coming? I, I, I—that was the problem! What an egotist I had become! Sure, I could accomplish. You bet my goal-finder worked, but I was on a new threshold and you will be, too, at some point. I had to learn that **to accomplish more I could not do it alone.**

This chapter is entitled "Change Opportunity to Reality" because that's exactly what we must do to change the imagined into the real. There is only so much we can do ourselves. There's only so much time available for our use. There's only so much brainpower, talent, drive, desire, experience and energy that you and I have to offer. We, then, are limited to what we can do **personally.** We must add something more to our mind power to success arsenal. Where do we get more of the same to use? From other people!

YOU MUST HAVE HELP TO ACHIEVE BIG GOALS

It took me nearly thirty years, the tragedy of a divorce, the pain of living aloof from others and tough times on the job to figure out something was wrong. Suddenly, nothing was going the way it was supposed to be going. I stopped to analyze the problem. Still, I couldn't see that I was trying to be the last of the individualists, the "I can do it myself" he-man.

In the process of trying to sort out myself, my wife, Kathy, came into my life and offered help. For the first time since I was a teenager, I accepted it. That was tough. You see, first I had to admit that I **needed** someone else's help. I had to accept that I could welcome into my life others' talents, energy and brainpower plus their desire, time and efforts given on behalf of what I was trying to achieve.

Now this acceptance seems only natural and right. Once I accepted help I could see new vistas. Wow—other people thinking with me! Concerned people with the same objectives in mind! People who have their goal-finders working on my behalf! This is terrific! All I have to do is get a **lot** of people thinking the same way—get all of their goal-finders working.

"Kathy," I said, "it's great having a partner who has the same objectives in mind. This is a real **first** for me."

"That's not exactly true, Bill," she replied. "You have an excellent example you're involved in every day and you haven't recognized it for what it is."

"What's that?" I asked, perplexed.

"The shop and your mother."

She was right. What an excellent example of an individual using her talents, abilities, energies and time to help a person change opportunity into reality. Here's how it happened:

I was buying rental properties, doing most things myself, when Ed Bush, a local real estate agent, asked me if I would be interested in buying a beauty salon. Well, that was way out of my line. I had been in the business of selling toilets, writing newspaper articles, broadcasting, dabbling in real estate; I had even been a soldier, but I had never considered curling hair.

ME? THE OWNER OF
A BEAUTY PARLOR?

"No, Ed," I answered, "not a beauty parlor."

You see, I was rejecting an opportunity that my goal-finder produced for me as a result of my objective to obtain wealth by buying real estate. Basically, I was rejecting the opportunity because I couldn't see how a beauty shop could be profitably managed. Then I sat down and began to imagine myself as the successful owner of the shop and, of course, the building that went with it. I imagined myself collecting additional rent from the upstairs apartment and much revenue from the beauty services. It was exciting! Remember, the brain doesn't know the difference between the imagined and the real. How would I control the employees? How would I buy supplies? How could I watch the business? Obviously, I could not. Yet the scene that I had imagined was so exciting that I found it impossible to give up the opportunity.

However, I wasn't convinced it could be done. I had to continue to travel for my company. I had to follow through on my growing commitments to speak for convention audiences. I had no time for a new venture. My thirteen rental units needed attention. Lakewood Park took time. I already had too much going on. Still, the opportunity was intriguing.

Can you relate to this? Are you at a point in your life where things are piling up? Are you at the end of your time, talent and energy rope? Then this chapter is for you—especially right now. Nothing complicated here; read on.

The opportunity of the beauty parlor persisted, and the idea of making it a reality intrigued me. But, I needed someone to help me. I thought of my mother. Would she be interested? We discussed it. Yes, she wanted the opportunity, and it happened!

Well, not that quickly. It took some negotiation, bank consultation, contract writing, etc. Before I was finished, I owned the real estate, the shop, the business, the supplies and had hired two hairdressers for what is now called The Glamour Boutique. And all was accomplished **without spending one penny** of my own money.

Remember, our point is that we are changing opportunity into reality and, in this case, it's accomplished by using another's talents and abilities. Mother and I established the operating procedures. I designed a small advertising program and helped monitor the start-up of the business under the new name and management. That was three years ago. One month after the business was started, it began to grow. Now there are six hairdressers, and it's one of the most successful shops in the county.

What a manager mother turned out to be! At fifty-eight, she schooled herself in the beauty business. She read textbooks, consulted supplier salespeople and learned from every source available. She fired poor performers and hired new help until she had what she wanted. She built our organization and increased volume by 50 percent the first year. She constantly monitored, planned, staffed, trained, motivated and supervised. She handled the books, taking care of both cash receivables and accounts payable. And what did I do? Well, after the first month, I relaxed. The business ran on the talent of another person. This sounds almost as if I used my mother to increase my wealth; well, the truth of the matter is I did. However, please don't judge me too harshly. You see, my mother wanted to work. She had been active all her life and no longer could work for the insurance company where she had handled a debit route. Her salary from the beauty shop gave her the luxuries she wanted, and the work became the delight of her life. She actually "lived" for the shop. Yes, she was getting what she wanted. And herein lies a fact: **To get what you want out of life, you must help others get what they want!** That's the secret I'd been missing all along.

So, Kathy was right. I had a perfect example right in front of me. I saw what it was possible to achieve by accepting the help of others. I also learned something else by accepting help: **Other people augment areas where I am deficient.**

MAKE UP FOR YOUR SHORTCOMINGS

My talents are special, but so are yours. When I ask you to help me and you agree, I gain talents you have that I do not. In this way I make up for my shortcomings. What an advantage! Other people can help you achieve your objectives; they can add to your time bank, your talent bank, your energy bank and can make you successful in ways that you can't imagine. Because another person managed the beauty shop, that business helped me improve my financial position in hundreds of ways and gave me time for other things. Since then I have enlisted the aid of many people who have become part of my life and I part of theirs. As I ask for help, I make sure in some way that **I also help them get what they want.** I give my talents to them as I

OTHER PEOPLE CAN HELP YOU ACHIEVE YOUR OBJECTIVES AND MAKE YOU SUCCESSFUL IN WAYS THAT YOU CAN'T IMAGINE.

borrow theirs. But overall I feel that I am the real winner as the diverse talents of these friends, in part, are added to my own storehouse of capabilities. I am thankful for these people who continue to teach me specialties. There's Frank Nuzzo, who's one of the most persistent people I know; John Amaser, who knows how to be a fearless charger; Janet Altobell, who is delightfully creative and brought the words of my first book alive with her illustrations; Bernie Thompson, who is logical and persuasive; Bob Carlson, who is the most honest person I know; and dozens of others who have added to the "me" that is incomplete without their help as I use more mind power for success.

Where are the people who will help you? Who are they? Why would they be interested in helping you? What can you give to them? Can you help them get what they want out of life? It will be important for you to answer these questions before you can move on to bigger and better accomplishments.

GETTING HELP TO CONVERT
OPPORTUNITIES TO REALITIES

What I'm really saying here is that most of your opportunities will lie dormant if you try to convert them by yourself. Some are just going to pass you by for lack of attention. Don't think you can go it alone. You can't. That's self-defeating and an exercise in futility. Besides, once you start working with people, enlisting their help, swapping talents with them and enjoying their company, your life becomes happier than it was when you tried to go it alone. You really need other people's help. Here's how to get it:

You have heard the word **motivation** used many times. Is it possible to motivate someone? Is it necessary that another be motivated to help you? Yes! That's the only way you can get the help you need. But motivation is like a bath: even though you take one today, you'll still need another tomorrow. You must become a full-time motivator in order to gain and keep the help you need to be successful. It is an ongoing process that must continue as long as you intend to continue your mind power to success program. This is indeed mind power as you become involved in influencing others to think along lines that will help you become successful. You must really get inside other people's heads to find out what they want out of life so that you can touch their hot button and get their attention. As you help them, they will be motivated to help you.

MOTIVATE OTHERS TO HELP YOU

What I am about to write does not fit the general academic descriptions of the motivation process, but the advice I give you here worked for me. Also, I have seen it work for others, and I know it will work for you.

I have had many people tell me that one individual cannot motivate another. They say that motivation is an internal, self-generated process. Well, that may be so, but I have proved over and over that the process of self-generated motivation is most often stimulated by **others.**

You see, the person who says an individual cannot be motivated by another is one who has failed in the attempt. Therefore, he is making excuses for his own lack of success. Probably that person failed in his attempts to motivate others because he never learned the techniques you are about to encounter. People tend to scoff at what they don't understand. You get "up" on the techniques of motivation! You become determined to employ others' goal-finders on your behalf. Beginning now, you practice learning more about other people and how to persuade them to become a part of your life in a positive, motivated way.

FROM MUNDANE EXISTENCE TO OUTSTANDING SUCCESS THROUGH MOTIVATION

Before we discuss the techniques of how to motivate others, I want to share comments from people who are dramatic examples of how individuals can be motivated to be on fire within a short period of time. These examples come from a controlled environment especially designed to accomplish just such a motivation. The motivational action occurred during my selling seminars.

One example was Pete Savas, a New England wholesale distributor salesman who came to my two-day workshop only because his boss told him he had to. Pete had already been seeking a job outside the field of selling because he felt he was a failure. The week before our session he was prepared to notify his company that he was quitting. However, following our seminar he said, "Before coming here, I had my doubts about being a salesman. I have always wanted to help people. I never thought that I could truly help someone by selling them a bill of goods. Now I see where I was wrong. There is more to gain in self-satisfaction in the sales business than in such a rewarding field as medicine. The doctor helps me, but then he is gone. I can help satisfy the needs of my customers on a continued basis. That really turns me on. I've found myself. I hope to stay as motivated as I have been in the past two days."

Up to that point, Pete Savas had been the poorest salesperson in his organization. Pete's hot button was his desire for an opportunity to help people the same way a social worker would. One of the points made during the seminar was that a salesperson had to be a need satisfier. This really hit Pete's hot button. He saw how he could be a customer's problem solver. He realized that the profession of selling gave an individual one of the finest opportunities to be involved in the people-to-people business. He was concerned, however, about his motivation lasting.

Well, since motivation is like a bath—necessary every day—I was also concerned about Pete and his daily self-motivation. So, I followed up on him and discovered Pete stayed motivated. He became the number one salesman for his company and today is a successful sales manager.

Sometimes it is difficult to use personal testimonials based on my experiences and my sales training sessions. However, I am trying to build a base of credibility for myself. I want you to know that I have been through this business of motivation. I have seen people with the personalities of manhole covers who suddenly turn around and catch fire because they are so motivated by an idea or a project. For example, another industry salesperson who wasn't motivated until he found his hot button in a selling principles and motivational seminar said, "Thank you for bringing some light to my attitude about selling. I enjoy my work and now feel that your concepts, when employed, will make my work a love story."

Another individual, who had been with his company for twelve years, was working daily in a nice, comfortable rut. He had this to say after he was stimulated by a sales training session, "This course has done many things. Primarily, it has reaffirmed that we are unique people and that with proper motivation and tools, we can have no limits to our sales success. Our minds are open, and we can jump as high as we want. Thank you for revealing more of us to ourselves."

Okay, enough of that. I just want you to know that I've helped others become motivated, and that motivation can be achieved on both a short- and a long-term basis.

DEAL WITH OTHERS AS INDIVIDUALS

People can be and will be motivated! In the case of Pete Savas, he just needed to know more about what he was doing. He needed to become "up" on his profession and himself so he would not be "down" on either. The same applied to the other individuals I quoted. Most people react the same. This is a key for you to get others motivated to help you. **Get them involved and show how it will benefit them.** By getting other people "up" on what you are trying to

THOUGHTS
OF THE
DAY
1____ 3____
2____ 4____

GET OTHER PEOPLE INVOLVED AND SHOW HOW THE INVOLVEMENT WILL BENEFIT THEM.

do and showing them how they will benefit, you are using two motivational hot buttons at the same time:

1. When people know all about what you are attempting to do and believe in your goals, they automatically are moved to help.
2. When people see benefits for themselves, they begin to "goal find."

But be careful. All individuals are unique and therefore must be handled differently in the motivation process. In fact, as you select people to help you with your mind power to success program, you must develop a system of elimination. You must be able to select people who can reinforce you in a positive way and eliminate those people who would bring negatives into your life.

I've found that there are four basic types of people that we must learn to relate to as we seek their aid and attempt to motivate some of them to be part of our mind power to success plans. I know from experience that you will find these descriptions to be true. The four types of people you will deal with include:

1. The perpetual skeptic.
2. The I-don't-care person.
3. The I-am-interested person.
4. The go-get-'em zealot.

The **perpetual skeptic** always projects the attitude of the unbeliever. This person cannot help you. You'll never be able to motivate him. You'll never be able to find his hot button. This person will constantly question your plans, ideas and strategies. He cannot imagine your goals being reached. He will always wonder what you are trying to do. When you get excited about something and share new ideas, he will have many reservations about the concept and why it won't work. He will have grave doubts about **anyone** ever being interested in you or your actions. He will laugh at your hopes for success. He will scoff at the entire concept of mind power to success, fill you with self-doubt and reduce your vision to a silly dream. He will never experience the real success of using his talents and abilities because he can never imagine himself in a self-fulfilling situation. If he can't see his own possibilities, he will never see the possibilities in you. Don't allow yourself to be influenced by the negative attitudes of this person.

The **I-don't-care person** is not openly hostile to your ideas, but he can pose an even greater problem. He is lukewarm about everything. To him your ideas will be just a variation of what he considers to be the same old thing. **To him, mind power to success will just be another name for old concepts.** This person will use clichés such as "There's nothing new under the sun" to justify his lack of interest. Because this individual is so indifferent, he is more difficult to inspire than the perpetual skeptic. He remains so detached from everything that he is in a perpetual state of apathy. Stay away from this person. He is dangerous to you and your mind power to success program. He will see your opportunities and shoot them down before you have a chance to make them a reality. You don't need this individual. You must not have this type of thinking as part of your subconscious programming. It will only hold you back.

The **I-am-interested person** provides an opportunity for you as you enlist the aid of others. This person can work with you in a paid capacity, either through wages or **psychic income.** By psychic income I mean the rewards achieved by being a part of something good. This person is not necessarily a self-starter, but will respond to good ideas. When you share an idea with this person, he will say that it sounds good and that he wants to learn more. He is willing to get "up" on the things he is down on and can be convinced of a new direction.

Work with this person. Ask for his help. He will grow with you. He'll want to hear and learn more. The more he learns, the more he'll become committed. He'll think there is value in your approach and will participate as fully as he can. He'll think that your ideas might give him a chance to achieve more in life. He'll see benefits for himself. Since he's also inclined to try new things, he'll want to be shown the way. With proper persuasion, this person can become genuinely enthusiastic over your plans and goals. Find him! Bring him into your confidence.

The **go-get-'em zealot** is rare, like an endangered species. Even after you find him, he is generally busy doing exactly what you are doing: working on his own mind power to success program! But when you team up with this person, things happen. He'll pick up your ball and run with it. In fact, he'll want to be out front most of the time. He always catches on quickly. He knows the name of the game and moves so fast he leaves others standing in his dust. This person will see great opportunity in what you are trying to do. He will believe your ideas are a stroke of genius and will say so. He will tend to be almost too optimistic in every situation. However, this is still an advantage because his enthusiasm is infectious.

SEGREGATE AND OPERATE

Now you must segregate the people you know and operate only with those who can help you. It does no good to waste your time trying to motivate people who are perpetually skeptical or who really don't care about anything. Think of the people around you and divide them into the four categories just discussed. **Do not make the mistake of letting relationships influence your decision.** There will be a tendency to put wives, husbands, fathers, mothers, sweethearts, close friends and relatives in the most favorable categories. This is a big mistake. Evaluate your potential success helpers based on their motivational potential not on your present relationship with them.

Even wives or husbands can fall into the two negative categories. If that's so, you must list them where they belong. I regret the truth of the situation, but you must face reality. You **cannot** be subject to the negative influences of other people and expect to be successful. Think about that. We are on dangerous ground here. The people who will tend to hold you back often will be those closest to you. I warn you, you must not let it happen. I did and it slowed my progress for many years. I thought everyone close to me wanted the same things I did. That was not true.

Earlier I mentioned my divorce and implied that it was the result of not enlisting the aid of others—especially my first wife. Well, that was partially true, but actually she did not share my vision. Now I clearly see that I should have listed her in category number two, as an I-don't-care person. However, every individual is entitled to play out his life's role the way he wants. The importance of this listing is that you must surround yourself with people willing to be motivated to help you with your mind power to success program. You cannot have any unwilling help or enemies in your camp. Your time with others must constantly give you positive reinforcement of your ideas, dreams and success plan. This means you are ready to spend more of your time with those people you have placed in categories three and four. It also means that you must spend less time with those who belong in categories one and two, or at least waste no time discussing your success plan with those individuals.

CREATE A BRAIN TRUST

You must know how your mind works to understand why mind power to success is your key to **more.** For this reason, we will explore that subject in Chapter 5. Be patient—it's coming. As this chapter on changing opportunity to reality ends, you must take one more action as you enlist the aid of others: You must create a **brain trust!** You must become involved with individuals you listed in categories three and four in such a way that you all coordinate your knowledge and efforts to achieve goals. You must share your ideas and get positive reinforcement from these people. **You must also help them to achieve their goals.**

You see, the more you are involved with these individuals, the greater the power you receive from their positive input will be. You will develop concrete plans, be encouraged to try new things and not fear risk. Your brain trust helpers will encourage and stimulate you to try new things. Your brain trust will be a part of your mind programming and will give you a tremendous boost as you gain more and more mind power to success.

POINTS TO REMEMBER

1. Review all that you have done so far; give yourself some positive reinforcement.
2. Look for help from others if you think your goal-finder is broken.
3. Know that you must have help in order to achieve big goals.
4. Know that to get what you want out of life, you must help others get what they want.
5. Be assured that other people will fill in areas where you do not have talent.
6. Learn how to motivate others to help you.
7. Be sure to deal with other people as individuals; show them how your project will benefit them.
8. Know that there are four types of people you must deal with: the perpetual skeptic, the I-don't-care person, the I-am-interested person and the go-get-'em zealot.
9. Create a brain trust that will reinforce your ideas.

CHAPTER

5

KNOW HOW YOUR
MIND WORKS

When I was eight years old I received a magic kit for Christmas worth about $1.50. However, over the past thirty years that kit has been both directly and indirectly responsible for helping me earn tens of thousands of dollars—more about that in Chapter 6. I refer to my magic kit now, though, because it was a seed I planted in my mind that grew and produced a harvest of paid speaking engagements for me. Yes, I reaped greatly from that magic kit seed, and you can sow your mind with thoughts that will yield great opportunities for you, too. You just have to understand how that marvelous mind of yours works.

THE $1.50 MAGIC KIT EVENTUALLY
PRODUCED THOUSANDS OF DOLLARS.

YOUR MIND IS LIKE A FERTILE FIELD

Putting seeds in your mind is similar to planting seeds in the earth. In time that thought seed will produce a harvest. How can you use this fact to further develop mind power? What value lies in the fact that we all work as gardeners when we sow the seeds of thought and reap the harvest of our action? I'll answer these questions shortly. First, I'll share an exciting moment with you that will help to illustrate my point.

In July 1972, I moved my family from New Hampshire back to New Castle, Pennsylvania. Selling toilets had become a very successful venture for me in New England. My company, which was headquartered in New Castle, decided I should use my techniques on a national level. Hence the relocation.

My family had never owned property, so I always dreamed of being able to look to the horizon and say, "See this, it's all mine!" My goal-finder was activated long before July 1972, the year my property-owning goal was reached.

In New Castle, I found the farm that fulfilled my mind's image of what it should be. I purchased the farm at a price that then seemed unreasonable. Along with the house, barn and acreage was an old tractor, a 6' brush hog mower and a set of plows.

The day we signed the papers, immediately after completing the transaction, I drove to the farm, gave the keys to the house to my wife and headed for the barn. I wanted to drive the tractor. And I did! I was still wearing my suit and tie along with a big uncontrollable grin as I put-putted up and down the 750' lane. "Look at Dad," my daughter Stacy said. "It's just like 'Green Acres' on TV." I was a bit embarrassed as she kidded me about the then popular TV comedy show about a city man who was ineffective and funny trying to be a farmer.

I've never had the time to learn to farm, but I still enjoy mowing the fields to keep the weeds in check. That first week, though, I did try to plow. It was like playing with a life-size toy for me. However, I made a mess of the field and had to have a neighbor, Jake Bachun, fix it and plant corn.

Suppose I had plowed properly, raked the field and planted corn myself, but after six weeks when the cornstalks were about 2' high I pulled them out of the ground and found beets clinging to their roots. I would have been so excited that I would have run around that farming community showing everyone my marvelous discovery.

" LOOK AT DAD . IT'S JUST LIKE `GREEN ACRES´ ON TV. "

What do you suppose those farmer neighbors would have said to me? Right, they would have said I was crazy and assured me that I moved into the wrong community. They would have laughed and said I'd never be a farmer. They would have let me know that I could not have planted corn and harvested beets from that planting. Why? **Because that is absolutely against the law of nature.**

We don't put carrot seeds in the ground and harvest lettuce—we can't harvest something different from what we plant. And here's the tie-in with the way the mind works: **Thought seeds produce a harvest of whatever we plant, just like crop seeds.** In this way, the mind is just like the field on my farm. When Jake planted corn, we got corn. I know this sounds very simple, but when I think of the things I've observed people planting in their minds, I know many of them must not realize the importance of this fact. We will reap whatever we sow. When we allow negatives and garbage to be planted in our minds, we will eventually produce a harvest of negatives and garbage as a result of this thought-seeding. So, in that way your mind is very much like the field that a farmer plants. And your mind is like that field in another way.

PLANTING CORN AND PULLING UP BEETS IS AGAINST THE LAW OF NATURE. YOUR MIND WORKS THE SAME WAY.

What is the purpose of planting a corn seed? Is it to grow another **seed** of corn? Of course not. The purpose of planting the seed is to grow ears of corn. The purpose of planting the field is to grow an entire crop. Your mind, again, works just like the field since it not only produces a similar item, but does so in abundance. Why else would we do the planting? Whatever you put in the mind, you will get out! This concept, perhaps, is one that is better expressed in terms of today's electronic, computerized world. Think of your mind as being like a computer and become familiar with the phrase "GI–GO." This is a term used by computer experts and it means: "Garbage In equals Garbage Out."

YOUR MIND IS LIKE A COMPUTER

When I was in high school in the late '50s I came across a book entitled *Cybernetics*. It was a relatively new study dealing with mechanical devices that were able to seek a goal that was preprogrammed into the mechanisms. (Please understand that the principles described in this early writing were strictly mechanical and predated today's microchip technology.) The author designed toys that would perform simple functions and correct their actions as they sought a particular goal. The experimenter/author built a mechanical rat that could find its way through a maze by trial and error, eliminating those directions that resulted in its being blocked. The mechanical rodent would seek right to left, forward and backward until it reached the end of the maze where an automatic prod tripped its "off" switch. The illustration below shows how the mechanical animal was set in motion and how feedback provided the information to alter its direction.

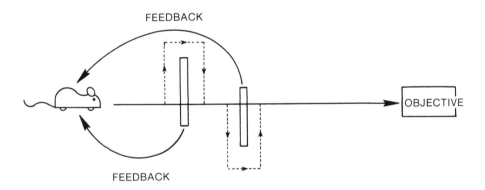

Keep this example in mind as we discuss how your mind is programmed in a similar way.

Is this feedback mechanism found in nature? Of course it is. You see it all the time. Consider the squirrel. Built into the squirrel's survival mechanism is the instinct to store food for the winter. What about birds? Do they have to take lessons in navigation? Look at the animal kingdom and you will see that creature by creature, animals have within them goal-finders that are automatic. Yes, they all have what I call built-in **automatic goal-finders,** or autogoal-finders. I've seen it. You've seen it. It is universal.

Why is it so difficult, then, for humans to accept that we have had autogoal-finders built into us, too? Discover your autogoal-finder and know that it is much more marvelous and complex than that of the animals.

YOUR MARVELOUS AUTOGOAL-FINDER

Animals are born with their autogoal-finders already set. They cannot select their goals because they are preprogrammed with a system that we call "instinct." You and I, on the other hand, have been endowed with the wonderful opportunity of using our imaginations to select various goals before our autogoal-finders are set into motion. We can set ourselves in any direction we wish, much like an airplane pilot who determines his course, makes adjustments on the way and arrives at his destination as planned.

Since I first read about cybernetics, science has come to the conclusion that the human brain and nervous system work together to become a tool for you to use in much the same way as you would one of today's computers. You have a built-in servomechanism that works as a guidance system to help you achieve goals. However, this doesn't mean that you can achieve success merely by thinking about it and then hoping that it will happen. Hoping by itself will not set your autogoal-finder in motion. You must work at programming your mind and allow sufficient time for your autogoal-finder to take control. A trip back to the farm will help explain this.

THE HORSES GOT SMARTER AS TIME WENT ON

About six months after buying the farm, I had the idea that I wanted to set off the front acreage with a white wood fence. I must have seen it in a movie or a picture because I had the image firmly set in my mind. I could see about seven acres in front of the house fenced in and visualized the mowed field setting off our home with its lush green grass.

I bought the fence posts and the wood rails, rented a fence post digger and enlisted the aid of my son to dig more than two hundred post holes. That was quite an undertaking. However, within two weeks the fence had been completed and painted a beautiful creosote white. About a week later, my daughter asked me why I had built the fence.

"Well, it's pretty isn't it?" I said.

"Yes, Daddy, but don't the other farmers use their fences for something?"

"Of course they do, Stacy, but we don't have any animals. You see, Janet Dean, next door, uses her barbed wire fence to keep in her cows."

"But, Daddy, can't fences keep in other animals, like horses?"

Of course they can. This was Stacy's way of asking for a horse, and we decided it was time to buy her one. Since she was only ten years old, I thought her horse should be a pony. We searched until we found one we thought was perfect. She named him Blaze.

It took Stacy about three weeks to discover that her horse was much smaller than the horses her friends rode. Soon we were looking for a larger animal. When we found Major, a beautiful buckskin quarter horse, she immediately fell in love with him. I thought he was a monstrous beast, but she had to have him because he had been a blue ribbon champion who'd won the barrel races at several local horse shows. Major became a member of the family, along with Blaze. Then, our older boy, Randy, decided he wanted a horse so he could go riding with his sister. His had to be a high-spirited Arabian. Soon, Smoke became the third member of our horse family.

Our other son, Billy, was raising chickens but wanted to get in on the horse act, too. We figured one more horse wouldn't really make much difference. Besides, ever since our children were small, we always tried to make our gifts to them as equal as possible. So, Billy sought and acquired Buck, whose name belied his gentle temperament. Next, their mother decided it might be a good idea to go riding with them, so we looked for a gentle mare for her. That's how Trudy joined our ever-growing stable of horseflesh.

One day I came home from work to be greeted by all three children who looked very concerned. They told me that a boy on a neighboring farm had a horse that was being mistreated. They coaxed me to go with them to see the horse on the pretext of giving the boy some advice about the animal. When I got there, a slow anger began to build inside of me. A shaggy, boney, ailing Appaloosa stood nearly motionless in a small paddock, obviously on his last legs. Several small children were using his neck as a sliding board; they were mounting his back and sliding forward until they tumbled to the ground. I wouldn't even shake hands on the deal as I shelled out cash to rescue the animal from his fate. I remember sitting up with this horse, named Warrior, until well past midnight, feeding him handfuls of grass and bits of grain in an attempt to gradually get some nourishment into his body. After several visits by the veterinarian and much tender loving care from the family, Warrior became a beautiful specimen. Best of all, he was mine! We had become a total horse-owning family.

Those were exciting days. We learned to ride, then we galloped through the fields and taught our horses to run the barrels, jump and perform other equestrian feats.

One day a young woman came to the farm asking if she could board her horse there. We decided we had room for one more. Besides, the stable fee would give us a little extra to help pay for the feed. However, one problem developed. After the young woman had ridden her horse for three or four weekends, she never came back again. When we couldn't locate her, we realized we had inherited her horse, Image.

As I look back on it now, I realize I was partially responsible for this horse insanity. But we dearly loved the animals and were willing to make sacrifices in order to keep them. Because of this, the number of our stable residents kept growing. One Saturday at an auction, Stacy spied a small colt that was to be put on the block. She had always wanted to train a horse from the time it was a colt. That's how Cocoa came into our lives. Now we had a grand total of eight horses. That was just too much.

On one of my trips, I gave the matter some thought. I had to take charge. I came home and told my family that we had overdone the whole horse venture. I told them that they had to have begun the process of selling the horses by the time I returned from my three-day trip. When I returned from my trip I discovered they had sold my horse! All I was left with was a silver studded parade saddle and a cowboy outfit.

Eventually, some form of reason set in and we reduced our stable to three horses. Now—to the point of this horse tale.

The real horsewoman in the family is Stacy. She taught us all something about horses and, ultimately, about ourselves and how our minds work. Over a period of two years I watched Stacy train each horse that we owned. She showed us that Blaze had a personality different from Major's and that Trudy was very skittish, whereas Buck would rarely react to anything. We learned Warrior was shy and took a long time to cozy up to any individual; the colt Cocoa was frisky, but seemed to love having people around. Image, the horse left by the young woman, never seemed to fit in with the others; he was always being chased away from the group—they made him graze at a distance of at least 25'. Smoke, the Arabian, took charge; he was the leader. Wherever he went, the other horses followed; when he did not desire their company, he chased them away. He was first in and first out of the barn. Yes, even horses have their individual personalities. What instinct nature gives them keeps them in the *Equus caballus,* or horse family, but their personalities make them individuals.

Beyond that individuality, Stacy pointed out something else to me. When we bought the colt, I explained to her that she would have to break him before she could ride him. "Oh, no, Dad," she said. "You don't break horses, you gentle them." And she showed me what she meant.

First, she tied the colt, Cocoa, to a tree and patted him and talked to him for several days. Then, she placed a blanket on his back. He promptly shivered and shook off the blanket. After several days, however, he allowed the blanket to remain. After that, she put grain sacks on his back so that he could feel additional weight. Thereafter, she led him around by the halter with this weight. Finally, she placed a saddle on his back and tightened the cinch. He even allowed this. In a matter of twenty-one days, going from one step to the next, she did, indeed, gentle that colt. By the time she mounted him and sat in the saddle, he was completely used to the idea that this was something that should be done.

In addition to the colt, Stacy taught the other horses skills that were well within their ability. This is where I learned the lesson: As long as each skill was taught very slowly and deliberately, the horse was able to acquire it within approximately twenty-one to thirty days.

At the time we also had two dogs. We tried to teach them tricks using the same principles Stacy used with the horses. We taught them very slowly and took approximately twenty-one to thirty days. It worked! However, we never succeeded with training the chickens.

What did I learn from this horse–dog–farm experience? I found that most animals who have built-in autogoal-finders can be taught to perform a particular feat within a period of twenty-one to thirty days. From this I figured that a normal learning cycle was approximately that time span. So, if we can teach new things to horses, dogs

IT TAKES TWENTY-ONE DAYS TO LEARN SOMETHING NEW. STACY LEARNED THAT BY TEACHING HER HORSES.

and other animals, we, as humans, can certainly teach ourselves new things. It's a matter of programming the mind, of realizing that there must be a certain amount of persistent input and practice that will allow us to acquire the skill until it's nearly automatic. With this in mind, I went back to my books and the study of cybernetics.

It was here that I discovered Maxwell Maltz and his book, *Psycho-Cybernetics,* first published in 1960. What a marvelous discovery that was! I learned from the book that when we select a goal and faithfully work toward it by practice, an automatic mechanism takes over so that enough practicing will eventually help us achieve the goal and then repeat it automatically without even thinking about it. I began to learn about the subconscious and how once we plant a thought seed into the mind we can reap an entire harvest from it. This is what I meant in earlier chapters when I said that we only do things well when they are programmed into the subconscious mind. That's where our autogoal-finder is located.

Once Stacy's horses repeated an activity several times over a period of twenty-one days, they performed that activity well. You and I do the same thing. When we perform an activity over and over, we are doing several things at the same time:

1. We are planting seeds in the mind regarding that activity.
2. In the sense of the computer, we are programming our mind so that we will get out of it exactly what we put in.
3. With each repetition or practice we are reducing the difficulty of the activity and committing it to the subconscious mind.

GET SET TO BEGIN PROGRAMMING

So, how does your mind work? Well, you can plant seeds and expect to grow a harvest of whatever you sow. This means you must be careful. It means that you will want to grow a beautiful predetermined crop and not a wasteland of weeds. Plant the thought seeds yourself.

Remember that your mind is very much like a modern computer. If you put garbage in, garbage will come out. So, beginning right now, change the computer formula GI–GO to mean: "Good In equals Good Out."

And know this about your mind: **Allow at least twenty-one days to program any new activity.** We learned the lesson from the horses, and we know from Maxwell Maltz that it takes time to have new ideas and concepts reach the subconscious level of our thinking. It's in this subconscious, as we will learn in Chapter 6, that we become experts at any endeavor. Since you now know how your mind works, let's set about programming it.

POINTS TO REMEMBER

1. Your mind is just like a fertile field.
2. Your mind is also like a computer.
3. You now know that you have an autogoal-finder.
4. You can program your mind in a twenty-one-day period.
5. Learning is very difficult, and you must continue to practice in order to do well.

CHAPTER
6
PROGRAMMING YOUR MIND

You are ready to take affirmative action that will catapult you to one success after another. You know how your mind works and now it's time to program it, set your autogoal-finder, energize your talents and make use of every precious second of your life so you can be what you want to be and have what you want to have!

This chapter on programming your mind will give you the how-to system that you need to learn new information and make that material part of your mind power to success program. You are on the threshold of growing at a more rapid pace than you ever have before. You are a mere twenty-one days away from the person you want to be. But, before you go on, make a commitment: Promise to read this chapter **six times** to make sure the concepts reach your subconscious mind. Also, decide to take action where you are directed to do so. That's all there is to it. Now, let's see how programming your mind will advance your mind power to success development.

THE KIT THAT WAS MAGIC

Remember the $1.50 magic kit I mentioned in Chapter 5, the one that eventually enabled me to earn tens of thousands of dollars? Well, it was really thought seed planting and follow-up mind programming plus the magic kit that made things happen for me.

Once I got the kit, I imagined myself performing in front of an audience of friends, neighbors and relatives. Do you see what happened? My creative imagining set my goal-finder for seeking ways to achieve that imagined scene. But just setting the goal-finder to work wasn't enough. It would have been impossible to immediately stand before a group and do magic tricks that would either amuse or entertain. I didn't have the knowledge or practical skill to pull it off.

There was an instruction book with the kit, of course, and I enthusiastically read over and over the directions in it. Still, I could not perform the tricks well just by reading the directions. I had to go one more step and practice. I had to go over every trick repeatedly, practicing in front of a mirror until each one looked like real magic. Only then had I actuated my autogoal-finder. Only after days and weeks of practice did I program the moves into my subconscious mind so that I automatically performed the sleight of hand necessary to create magic while, at the same time, I talked to my audience, telling stories known as the magician's "patter."

THE $1.50 MAGIC KIT ENABLED ME TO SPEAK IN FRONT OF CONVENTION AUDIENCES. YOU MUST PROGRAM YOURSELF TO TAKE ADVANTAGE OF PREVIOUS SUCCESSES.

Was there success? Yes. But, that's not so important. Many young boys did magic tricks. The importance of this story is what developed after I became an amateur magician—I learned to speak before groups. The patter necessary to perform magic well taught me to relate to audiences at a very early age. This skill was programmed into my mind so that it had become easy for me to do.

Later, when asked to present sales meetings and still later, when asked to speak before convention audiences, even though I felt the fear of the moment I was prepared because my mind had long ago been programmed to relate to an audience as a public speaker. Now I don't have to worry about technique—it's there. I can concentrate on the content of the message and trust my programmed skills to deliver the material in a digestible form. Programming should not be new to you because you are doing it every day. The problem is **it's not controlled.**

Remember the statement in the first paragraph of Chapter 1? I told you that you will not be the same tomorrow as you are today. I said that within sixty seconds a change would begin. I was programming your mind. Throughout these pages I have continued the process. I've used repetition, telling you in many ways to set goals, think of yourself as successful, make victory lists of things you have done well, know you are special, dwell on your talents and abilities, enlist the help of others, change your opportunities into realities—all as a matter of programming your mind with a new vocabulary and new concepts. You have already changed because your mind has been expanded with this information and **the expanded mind never returns to its former shape!** Now, I'm dedicated to accelerating your progress.

YOU HAVE THE POWER OF A MARVELOUS MENTAL DEVICE

Imagine that all the computer technology existing today was gathered in an effort to build the most advanced computer in the world. The object of this project would be to duplicate all of the functions of the human brain. The experts tell us it would take a building the size of the Sears Tower in Chicago to house such a computer, even in these days of microchip systems. Even then, however, this project would not duplicate the creative functions of the human mind. What a wonderful device you have at your beck and call. What power!

Often I have heard physicians say that a large percentage of illness is psychosomatic; that is, the aches, pains and other symptoms of sickness are caused by an individual's imagination. Doctors who suspect such a condition often prescribe placebos, or sugar pills, to take care of the imaginary ills. And, they work. Even cases of severe skin rash, bad headaches, back pain, stomach ailments— illnesses that were not imaginary at all—have been cured with placebos. The mind imagined that the effects of the pills would be a cure and the body responded, in each case, to these expectations. Imagination caused an actual physical reaction. Mind power cured the patients.

HE LAUGHED AT A TERMINAL ILLNESS

I saw a "60 Minutes" program a couple of years ago that featured a man who had been told three years earlier that he had an incurable blood disease and only six months to live. However, to the amazement of specialists in the field, his disease had disappeared. How did it happen? What did the man do to cure himself? **He laughed himself well.**

HE LAUGHED HIMSELF WELL.

The man read that our body chemistry changes when we laugh so he decided to put as much humor into his life as he possibly could. He had his wife rent Abbott and Costello movies and bring them with a projector to his hospital bedside. He watched them along with cartoons, Charlie Chaplan and Laurel and Hardy movies and other films that provoked belly laughs. Soon he felt so good he was released from the hospital. He continued the process at home. He read joke books and thought of every funny incident that ever occurred in his life. He continued to feel better and within six months, supposedly all the time he had left, he was entirely cured. That, too, is mind power! It's also programming.

YOU MUST BELIEVE

Your belief, your imagination in action, is the first step to having what you want. In order to use your mind you must put something into it to work on and you must believe in the result you are trying to achieve. Placebos work because the patients **expect** them to work. I believe the laughter cure worked because the patient **expected** it to work. Your programming will work when you, too, **expect** it to work.

Remember, your subconscious mind does not know the real from the imagined and, therefore, will act on the information it receives. If you keep imagining something you will eventually act according to what you imagined. Behaviorist psychologists tell us that we eventually develop attitudes based on our actions. What they mean is that when we perform an act often enough we will eventually believe in that particular action. Now, since the subconscious mind cannot determine whether or not the act is real, even imagined acts can help develop new attitudes. Based on what we have learned so far, how long do you suppose it would take new attitudes to develop based on new actions? If you're thinking twenty-one days, you're right. Every day that you spend imagining a goal, a cure or a desired result gives positive reinforcement to your autogoal-finder mechanism and your entire being reacts to the belief as if it were so.

IT'S A MATTER OF HYPNOTISM

While in college, I developed my magic show to include not only tricks with silk scarves and floating lady illusions, but also a segment

THE SUBCONSCIOUS MIND DOES NOT KNOW THE REAL FROM THE IMAGINED AND, THEREFORE, WILL ACT ON INFORMATION IT RECEIVES. THIS WAS SEEN DURING MY HYPNOTISM SHOWS.

on mind reading and hypnotism. In fact, this became the most popular part of the program. Even today I occasionally present a program entitled "Experiments in ESP." I learned a lot about the human mind as a hypnotist. Most of the demonstrations were for stage entertainment, but later I used the same techniques while working with medical doctors interested in treating their patients through posthypnotic suggestion.

Hypnotherapy worked the same way as the placebo effect. We were able to capture the imagination of the patient and under the direction of the physician, I used suggestion to program the subconscious mind. I worked only as a tool, the operator. The patient did the actual hypnotizing by following my suggestions. This is a very powerful tool because it reaches the subconscious mind and immediately programs it to respond. To illustrate the potency of hypnotism and the power you have in your subconscious that hypnotism activates, here are some examples:

1. **Sensation is controlled by the mind.** A hypnotized person can be told that he is either hot or cold and will react according-ly. If told he is hot, he will perspire and want to shed some clothing. If told he is cold, he will shiver and goose bumps will form on his skin. This is the subconscious mind believing and reacting to control the body.

2. **Pain can be induced or removed.** Many dentists are using hypnotism instead of chemical anesthetics. The mind believes what the dentist says and blocks the pain. In my own experi-ments I placed a piece of metal in a subject's hand and had the person concentrate on it while I told him that it was growing warmer and warmer. Then I suggested it was getting so hot that it was impossible to hold. To the delight of the audience, the subject yelled "Ouch" and dropped the metal. This experiment was in all my shows until one evening a subject developed a blister on the palm of his hand. His body had reacted to the pro-gramming. The mind perceived the hot metal as real and sent a message to the hand which reacted physically and blistered. I learned a lesson. I never did that experiment again or any that could have possibly caused a natural physical reaction.

3. **Habits can be broken.** Today, doctors are hypnotizing their patients to break old habits and establish substitutes, to repro-gram away from the bad and toward the good. Many medical doctors are also using hypnotism to help patients lose weight or stop smoking.

4. **The subconscious can control activities.** Also in my shows, I would hypnotize audience members and have them sell imagi-nary newspapers or fish in an imaginary pond with an imagined fishing rod. Even though the audience roared with laughter, these subjects seriously went about their tasks, their autogoal-finder clearly set in motion, their subconscious mind in control of their activities.

5. **The mind responds to posthypnotic suggestion.** While a person is hypnotized, his mind can be programmed to respond to a certain cue after he awakens. This is known as post hypnot-ic suggestion. The person wakes up, hears the cue, responds to it but doesn't know why. He responds because his subconscious mind was programmed that way.

Basically, all of this means three things:

1. The hypnotic approach is very, very powerful.

2. You have been hypnotizing yourself into and out of things all your life.
3. You can monitor the hypnotic influences of your life and there-fore control this wonderful power.

YOU MUST DEHYPNOTIZE YOURSELF

Many things you do are a result of having hypnotized yourself into believing they are right. You may be wrong; you may be routinely performing acts that are holding you back. Your actions may be working in reverse, using your mind power to pull you away from success, not propel you toward it. You may not be aware that it is happening, just as the hypnotized subject in my show sold news-papers that to him were real. He was accomplishing nothing, but thought he was engaged in productive activity. It's in this sense that many people confuse mere activity with accomplishment. They are not the same. You can be extremely active but still not be accom-plishing anything toward your objectives if your activity is the result of counterproductive beliefs.

The following are examples of people who have programmed themselves in the wrong direction to believe in objectives that are counterproductive to what they want out of life:

- The manager who keeps looking over his employee's shoulder is not a manager; he is a checker.
- The wife who pays attention to the children and ignores her husband is only a mother. She could eventually lose her husband.
- The workaholic husband/father who comes home only on week-ends is just a paycheck. All his activity (work) will eventually be counterproductive to his real goals with his wife and children.
- The teenager who wants to be popular runs around with a burned-out crowd because they get a lot of notice. He is pro-gramming himself with antisocial behavior that will make it diffi-cult to function later in society.

Don't fall into these traps. If you're in one now, get out! You can. Begin a program of dehypnotizing yourself away from the counter-productive and hypnotize yourself toward achieving the productive. Start by finding the cause of your situation. Look at the following diagram:

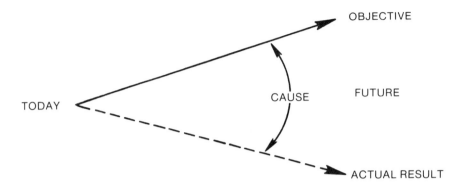

This little visual is to help you focus on where you are and to help you set a new direction. At the left you can see where you are **today**. You can also see where you are headed if there is no change in your activities—**actual result**. At the same time you can see where you want to be—**objective**. The diagram shows **cause** separating you from **objective**. As you move further from **today** toward **future,** the **cause** becomes bigger and bigger. This **cause** is the counterproductive programming that results in counterproductive activities. You become more and more hypnotized into this negative programming the more you persist in using it.

You must change the **cause** to achieve your **objective.** You must change your behavior in order to affect your attitudes and reprogram your subconscious mind. The more time that passes, the further you will move away from where you want to be.

Do you believe this to be true?

The way you answer that question will determine whether or not you are ready to use the power of the hypnotic process to deprogram and reprogram your mind for success. You see, even when hypnotized, a person will not perform acts that are against his nature. It would not be possible, for instance, to tell a hypnotized person to commit a violent act if it was against his will to do so. Such a suggestion would be so uncomfortable for the person that he would awaken. An individual must believe in the concepts presented, and the concepts must be acceptable to his basic nature.

When you believe what has been discussed in this chapter, you can easily begin the process of positive change to get where you want to be and have what you want to have. This is the reason I asked you to commit yourself to reading this chapter six times. I want this information programmed into your subconscious so you will be virtually hypnotized into responding positively to the message contained here. Now, let's discuss briefly the process of dehypnotizing.

WHY DEHYPNOTIZE?

You cannot continue in your old ways and expect to develop a new you. To become the person you want to be you must get rid of old concepts and change your actions. You must take action **now!** For years people believed that if attitude could first be changed then behavior would automatically adjust. Not true. Your behavior will lead you to new attitudes. Your present attitude is merely a confirmation of your behavior, a rationalization of what you do.

If, for instance, social conditions forced you to behave as if you believed in theft, you would eventually develop attitudes that would conform to that behavior; i.e., you'd approve of stealing. You would associate with others who stole for a living. Your attitude would develop into an autogoal-finding action in your environment and you would eventually choose to operate in an arena or segment of society where your behavior was acceptable. (Birds of a feather flock together.) You'd be reinforced by others engaged in the same activities and would develop behavior that would lead to new attitudes to support your activities. You'd then build a system of attitudes to confirm your behavior and from this develop your value system. Your value system would feed back confirmation for your behavior. Isn't this what happens inside our penitentiaries when first-time offenders come out "educated"?

But, let's not be negative. All of this works for good for you. What will determine your behavior from this point will depend on your talents and what your immediate environment will permit you to do. These are the only restrictions that you have. And they are not so much restrictions as they are opportunities as discussed in Chapters 1, 2 and 3.

GET RID OF BAD ATTITUDES BY GETTING RID OF BAD BEHAVIOR

Stop doing the things that are counterproductive! If you delay changing your counterproductive behavior, the change will be more difficult later. Some people wait until their forties or fifties to begin changing direction. That's okay, but the impact of such reprogramming can often be devastating to others around them. Often these people who change are considered to be having a mid-life crisis as they go after entirely new life-styles. But they find it impossible to change within the constraints of their current environment because there are so many influences programming them to maintain their status quo. These influences have built up over the years. It is not always possible to change everything around you, but it is possible to change the impact your environment has on you by adjusting to doses of various exposures. The world is basically negative and when you partake of it you are subject to being influenced by the negatives. Many people in today's society are so ingrained with negatives that their only means of feeling good about themselves is to act as if they are better than everyone around them. They constantly put down others in order to build up their self-image. These people should be avoided whenever possible.

CHANGE PHYSICALLY

A part of reprogramming is to change physically—this means doing something about your appearance. Take a good look at yourself. Are you satisfied with the way you look? Are you dressing the way you should? Are you overweight? Do you need help in the area of general fixing up? These areas are very important. In order to go up, you must dress up. Because your success depends upon relating to the rest of the world, you must present yourself as if you are a successful person. Improving your appearance will make you feel better and change your attitude.

IS THE GLAMOUR BOUTIQUE A HEALTH CLINIC?

Women leave our beauty shop, The Glamour Boutique, feeling much better than they did when they entered. It's what they see in the mirror that does the job. Many women who come into the beauty shop are depressed, unmotivated, even grouchy. Most of them exhibit all of the symptoms of defeat. They don't feel good about themselves and spend a good deal of time telling Kathy how everything is going wrong. Kathy is a good listener and sympathizer. She knows that within forty-five minutes all of that will change. They will leave feeling good about themselves again. Why? Because after their hair is done, they look into the mirror and see themselves differently. Our beauty shop does not sell only hair spray or perman-ent wave solution. These products can be bought in any discount drugstore. Our shop sells image. When the customer looks good that customer feels good and the entire world seems to be much, much better. When convinced that our shop or one of the hairdressers is the only one who can accomplish this transition, the customer will come back. If a customer no longer believes in the shop's capabili-ties, then that customer will find an image change elsewhere.

I worked as a clerk at the Babcock-Wilcox Company in my early twenties, but wanted to be an executive. When I worked as a clerk, I dressed like a clerk. When I went looking for a new job, I dressed like an executive. In a short time I found a new company and a new job that fit the image I had created.

Mary Kay Cosmetics is a modern day tale of what programming can mean. I saw her success story on the TV program "20/20." Of

THE GLAMOUR BOUTIQUE IS NOT A HEALTH
CLINIC, BUT WOMEN FEEL BETTER AFTER
THEY LEAVE BECAUSE THEY ARE
DRESSING UP TO GO UP.

course, Mary Kay representatives sell cosmetics, but Mary Kay does the real sales job of selling representatives on themselves. She presented an opportunity to prospective representatives that enabled them to imagine they were selling Mary Kay products and becoming financially independent. Supported by testimony of those who had already achieved, they believed and went after duplicates of those successes. In the process, they got rid of their negative self-images, changed their behavior, developed new attitudes, dehypnotized themselves and programmed themselves to become what they wanted to be and have what they deserved to have.

120 BEATS A MINUTE DOES THE JOB

Programming does work! There are hundreds of thousands of examples in everyday life. Some are positive, some are not. During the process of exposing yourself to new experiences and taking new action, you must be very, very careful. Remember, the influences of the world are hypnotizing us into and out of things every day.

When we ran the disco for teenagers, I noticed that the dancers were moving as if they were hypnotized. Having had some experience with hypnotism, I recognized the general fixed stare and the rhythmic action of the dancers moving to the music. It suddenly dawned on me that the disco music was, indeed, very hypnotic. The music was played at 120 beats per minute. This rate is extremely hypnotic to the human mind and enables suggestion to be planted very easily into the subconscious. Then, I decided to listen to some of the lyrics. I was shocked to learn that the artists were advocating hallucinogenic drugs, sex, and an "anything goes" behavior. This garbage was being programmed into the minds of 500 young people in my dance hall every Friday and Saturday night! Probably what I did helped thin out the crowd, but I began to audition all of the records and eliminated 40 percent of them. I still remember how upset I was about the music.

Several months later, I addressed the graduating class of a local high school. During the speech, I said that as we go into the world we must be very careful about what we allow to be programmed into our minds. I said that young people form their value systems based on the input they receive from their environment. I talked about disco music, alcohol, drugs and pornography and how having this material

THE DANCERS MOVED AS IF THEY WERE HYPNOTIZED. THE INFORMATION THEY RECEIVED IN THEIR MINDS WENT DIRECTLY TO THE SUBCONSCIOUS.

dumped into the mind or body will result in a harvest of garbage and negative attitudes will develop from the negative thought seeds that are planted. The speech was well received, particularly by the parents. I do very distinctly remember, however, one graduate coming up to me afterward and saying, "Mr. Stiles, I enjoyed your talk very much, but I have a question for you. Do you know any teenagers who produce those records?"

"No, I don't," I replied.

"Well, do you know any teenagers who own beer distributorships that make the beer so available to us? Any teenagers who own the movie houses that show the porno films? Any teenagers who own the publishing companies that produce the material you are talking about?"

Of course, I had to answer, "No." In fact, I knew the local businessmen who were responsible for making these materials available to the young people. Since then, my speeches regarding these activities have been delivered to the Lions, Rotary and other service clubs in the area. The young man who approached me after this session was essentially telling me this: When you point your finger at another person, notice how your hand is formed—when one finger is extended there are three others pointing back at you.

Of course, he didn't say it that way, but he was letting us know that the seeds we plant in the minds of our young people are those that we, as adults, are responsible for putting there.

In this brief aside in this chapter on programming, I give you a little message in the form of a plea—as you are changing your own life, pay attention to those around you. Try to accept some responsibility for what's happening in society. Absorb this message, carry it to two other people and ask them to do the same. In this small way, you and I can be influential in getting things turned around. As you take responsibility for yourself, also take responsibility for some of the rest of the world.

A little boy and his father were watching television one evening. The boy was bored with the program and told his father that he wanted something to do. The father was interested in the show, but wanted to accommodate his son. He quickly took a piece of newspaper and tore into several dozen pieces a page with a picture of a world globe. The man asked the boy to see if he could put the picture back together before the program ended. The little boy set about the task with enthusiasm. Of course, the father assumed that it would take some time for his son to reassemble the newspaper page, but to his surprise, the boy finished within ten minutes. The father asked his little boy how he was able to do that so quickly. The boy said, "There was a picture of a man on the other side of the page. All I had to do was put the man together and the world was together, too."

That's the way it is. If we can each put ourselves together, then automatically the world will come together, too.

GET YOUR FORWARD MOMENTUM GOING

Programming your mind is not as difficult as the length of this chapter might indicate. What the length does indicate is the degree of importance that I place on this concept. The ease of programming the mind comes once you finally start. When you get going you have momentum working for you. Once you have something in motion, it's just a matter of applying a little bit of pressure to keep it going. You've noticed this if you've ever had to push any kind of a vehicle. After you got it going, it rolled rather easily. The same applies to a task that isn't necessarily pleasant. Once you get to it, the going is much, much easier. Remember that any object in motion tends to

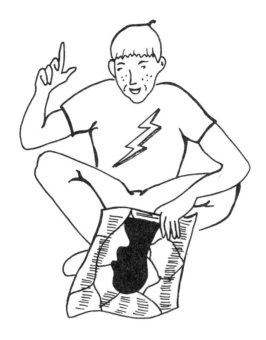

"THERE WAS A PICTURE OF A MAN ON THE OTHER SIDE OF THE PAGE. ALL I HAD TO DO WAS PUT THE MAN TOGETHER AND THE WORLD WAS TOGETHER, TOO."

stay in motion and it takes an opposite force to stop it. The same thing is true about objects that are at rest. It takes considerable force to get them started, but much less to keep them going.

Backward momentum in life tends to work the same way. If you are going backward, it's much harder to stop the momentum and start forward. That means it will take extraordinary effort on your part to reverse those things in your life that are going in a direction opposite from where you want them to go. But remember, once you turn them around you'll have to apply a little bit of pressure to keep them going. In fact you'll notice that other people will begin to reinforce your change in direction because they will comment on it. Just a little suggestion—when they ask what has happened to you, reply honestly and directly. Tell them it's the **new you.** This will commit you to your new direction and help you reach your goal.

BE SURE TO REDUCE YOUR NEGATIVE PROGRAMMING

You must reduce the amount of negatives that are planted in your mind today and every day of your life. This means that you have to begin now to change your exposure. How many hours are you exposed to television shows that program many negatives into your mind? Statistics show that television exposes society to tens of thousands of killings and other violent acts in a person's lifetime. Before television, people had never been visually exposed to that type of thing. This exposure has to contribute to the acceptance of violent behavior if not to the overt action. You may want to substitute programs with positive information that can prove beneficial to your overall goals. Many people chuckle when they know that another individual is an avid viewer of public television. But these people who laugh are often missing some of the best shows on the air today. Another way of replacing some of the negative television programming is with books. Also, video discs provide selective viewing and the cost of the equipment is decreasing almost daily.

Once you have started programming your mind, your education must never end. You must never completely graduate from your mind power to success school. You should be continually growing and periodically having graduation ceremonies for yourself as you accomplish your victories. Your little victories will eventually become bigger victories and the graduation ceremonies can become bigger ceremonies.

HE DIDN'T THINK I WAS "WRAPPED TOO TIGHT"

Let me reinforce this. When you begin to change, others will notice. In general, you will be out of step with society. Don't let this bother you, though; you are becoming a new and better individual. I've had my bouts with others thinking that I was out of step.

For example, several years ago, a co-worker of mine noticed that I was different. In fact, because of all my activities such as lecturing, writing, presenting entertainment shows, etc., this person said rather cruelly that he didn't think I was "wrapped too tight." My initial response was to be angry, but I realized that in relation to the rest of my little business community, I must have appeared to be "weird William." Of course, I didn't let that comment or others bother me. I continued along the path that I believed was right for me.

Ten years after he made that comment, this individual retired. He called and asked me if I would speak to his senior citizens' group. I told him I would be happy to. Following my talk, that man came up to me with tears in his eyes to say that my speech was the best message his group had ever received. I don't suppose he remembered the comment he had made about me a decade earlier. Of course, I didn't remind him of it, either. But I know this: If I had not continued along the path that I had set ten years earlier, my message never would have been delivered because I would not have grown enough for the invitation to have been extended to me.

Even though others may think you are "weird" at first, eventually they will see you as that exceptional person with mind power to success.

THE MAN WHO THOUGHT I WASN'T WRAPPED TOO TIGHT WAS MOVED TO TEARS OVER MY SPEECH. DON'T LET PEOPLE TURN YOU AWAY FROM YOUR OBJECTIVES.

KATHRYN HULME AND THE NUN'S STORY

People will try to stop you from attempting anything different because they will consider what you want to do as strange or even impossible. I know that fact all too well.

While serving in the United States Army in Germany, I worked as a legal clerk. I had an interest in writing and decided to write a history of the area where we were stationed. It was an old Nazi ski camp that had been untouched by the war. I discovered that immediately following the war the camp had been used as a haven for displaced persons. After that it was used as a camp for United States soldiers. When I was there in the early 1960s, the camp was used to house the Fifty-fourth Engineering Battalion.

During one of my evenings at the library, I came across a book about the Wildflecken Camp by Kathryn Hulme who had written *The Nun's Story* which became a best-seller and later was made into a motion picture. I decided that I wanted to write an updated piece on Wildflecken for the *Stars and Stripes,* the military newspaper in Europe. I wanted to use much of the information in Kathryn Hulme's documentary about Wildflecken when it was a displaced persons' camp because she had been there at the time. I'd read her book *The Wild Place* at least a dozen times and felt the history of what had been there twenty years prior to my visit. I became hypnotized by the story. I walked in the woods and saw the old Nazi bunkers that had been built to protect the camp when it was a ski training center. I imagined myself being there shortly after the war. I was so enthusiastic about the article I wanted to write, I talked to several of my soldier friends and told them that I was going to write to Kathryn Hulme and ask if she had any pictures I could use in my story.

Another example of "weird William" in action. Yes, others laughed at me. I remember one sergeant telling me that I was out of my mind. He said that even if Kathryn Hulme were still alive, she would not respond to a letter from a soldier in Wildflecken, Germany. But that didn't stop me.

I got the name of the publisher on the back of *The Wild Place* and wrote to Kathryn Hulme explaining what I wanted to do and asking if she had pictures. I told her I would return them along with a copy of the article after it was published. She replied within two weeks. She not only sent pictures, but her letter was also filled with emotion as she started with, "What a wonderful voice out of the past you are... ."

Not only did I get the pictures I wanted, but I had also given Kathryn Hulme a bit of pleasure during what turned out to be the last year of her life. She was delighted to receive word from someone living in Wildflecken. The time she'd spent there from 1945 to 1947 working with displaced persons was a very important part of her life.

I wrote the article and it was read all over Europe. And something else happened. Because of that article, I was made the battalion information officer and published my own newspaper which won an award for being the finest newspaper in competition with the Army, Air Force, Marine Corps and Navy; I was awarded an Army Commendation Medal for my service in Germany, the highest peacetime award for meritorious service. All because I **believed** in an idea. So don't worry if people laugh at your change. You are becoming someone special.

NOT ONLY DID I GET THE PICTURES I WANTED, BUT I HAD GIVEN KATHRYN HULME A BIT OF PLEASURE AS WELL.

As I write about how other people will affect your life, a message from my father pops into my mind as it does whenever I am faced with new challenges. It's not a very long message and I doubt if Dad really knew the impact that it had on me. He never told me much about how to do anything; he merely said that he knew I would be doing it. From time to time he would look at me, smile and say, "Bill, I see in you the ability to rise above the masses." That was quite a general statement, but in all of its generalization I knew that it applied specifically to me. The result of his statement, repeated periodically, helped to set my autogoal-finder in action and energized me to accomplish in many ways.

I say the same to you in a general way because after looking at the world and realizing there's nothing out there but mediocrity, I say that you, too, can rise above the masses. Don't let anybody laugh at an idea you have. That idea is a seed of greatness. You are one of a kind. You have special talents and abilities that nobody else has. All you have to do is program that talent and ability in such a way that you use your mind power for success.

HOW TO MAKE THE GRASS GROW GREENER

Remember Chapter 5 and the acres I fenced in? I wanted green grass, but that front field was nothing but weeds. Today, however, it is lush and green just like I saw in my imagination. Here's what happened. I cut down the weeds and the shorter grass grew. I cut this grass and the new growth was finer and greener. I continued to cut and each new growth was improved. Now it's a beautiful field. The same thing happens with us as we cut out the weeds in our life and allow the lush green grass of positive thoughts to grow. We must **take action** to constantly reinforce ourselves in a new direction and rid ourselves of behavior relating to the old.

There had to be some small grass plants under the weeds in order for the field to grow green. Had there not been, I would have had to do some replanting. That's the same way with you. If you have nothing with which to replace your former behavior, you are going to have a tough time succeeding. At the same time you stop the counterproductive activities, replace them with new productive ones. In this way you will eventually dehypnotize yourself away from the bad and rehypnotize yourself into the good.

This means that you have to reach out for new information. You have to allow time to reprogram. You have to take physical action to eventually have your behavior change your attitudes and, finally, your entire life. You will be attacking the **cause** of where you are and changing that to get where you want to be. Use books! Use other people's lives as examples! Use television! Use cassette tapes! Use video discs! All of these wonderful tools are available to you. Just think what would happen if your subconscious mind was constantly programmed with good, powerful information using these systems for twenty-one days! You couldn't resist changing. You would become the new you that you want to be.

By reading this book thus far you have already begun to take action. Your action has led to an attitude change. Now take further action. Listed in the chart below are books that will help you with your programming for mind power for success. Go to your library and check out some of these books.

A Set of Encyclopedias for Mind Power for Success	
Title	Author
Acres of Diamonds	Russell Conwell
Applied Imagination	Alex Osborne
Believe	Richard Devoss
Born to Win	James T. Jongeward
Dress for Success	John T. Molloy
How to Get Along with Almost Everybody	Elton Reeves
How to Stop Worrying and Start Living	Dale Carnegie
How to Win Friends and Influence People	Dale Carnegie
Human Engineering	Cavett Roberts
Laws of Success	Napoleon Hill
Looking Out for #1	Robert Ringer
Men Who Shaped America	Robert Flood
Profiles in Courage	John F. Kennedy
Psycho-Cybernetics	Maxwell Maltz
Schools without Failure	William Glasser
See You at the Top	Zig Ziglar
Self-Love	Robert Schuller
The Greatest Salesman in the World	Og Mandin
The Heart of a Champion	Bob Richards
The Home Team Wears White	Gary Warner
The Magic of Thinking Big	David Schwartz
The Power of Positive Thinking	Norman Vincent Peale
Think and Grow Rich	Napoleon Hill
Your God Is Too Small	J. B. Phillips

You'll have a dynamite package that will open a new world to you. You will shortly overcome a problem many people have when they set about developing their mind power to success—they lack information. There's nothing wrong with that. This is the reason that books are written. Look at the list again. Have any of the books been used in your school? Probably not. You and I were never exposed to the information between the covers of these books during our most formative years. This is why we flounder and become hypnotized by the negative aspects of society rather than programmed by the wonderful human engineering information contained in this collection of success books. **You now have a set of encyclopedias for mind power to success!**

USE MODERN DAY TECHNOLOGY FOR ACCELERATION

Often I am asked to present a seminar on material I have not organized into a seminar format. Usually I have very little time for preparation. I don't like to speak from notes because I feel if I can't remember the material, I have no right expecting others to remember it. How do I learn the subject matter? I use a tape recorder to program it into my mind. I hypnotize myself and reach the subconscious. I force-feed myself until I know it cold.

I read the information that must be presented and record the ideas. Then I listen to the tapes while driving, while taking a bath or even while watching television. Once I have been exposed to the information at least six times, I have it! It's mine! I can conduct my sessions and add impromptu comments, adjusting to the needs of my audience. You can learn the same way. Much material is already taped. You can buy cassettes by many of the authors in the suggested reading list. You can also make your own cassettes of your goals and what you are going to do to achieve them. Try it. Give yourself the opportunity to listen to your goals for a week or two. You'll feel strongly reinforced and will be hypnotizing yourself in the right direction. Try this program for one month:

1. Buy at least one good motivational tape series. (I recommend the Zig Ziglar "How to Stay Motivated" series.) Listen to these tapes at least six times.

2. Record your victories on tape and listen to the tape once a day for thirty days.
3. On the flip side of your victory tape, describe yourself as you want to be. While listening to this description, close your eyes and visualize a television screen. The program is what is being described on your audio tape. See yourself role-playing what is being said on the tape. Your mind will perceive those activities as being real and you will further hypnotize yourself to reach for those goals.

ARE YOU IN ACTION?

I asked you to make a commitment to action at the beginning of this chapter. The reading and the taping is a part of that action. Be faithful to this action and you will notice a change after several weeks of programming. Don't be discouraged if some things don't turn around as quickly as you want them to. Since you live at the center of your own universe, your reasons for change are sometimes wrong and won't work within your environment. Don't panic! This is just for a few of the things you try. In the balance, however, your successes will greatly outdistance your failures.

Do I fail? You bet. I probably have had more failure than most people have made attempts. How often you fail is not important. How long you persist and how you handle failure are what count. Now read on to find out why you should rejoice in failure.

POINTS TO REMEMBER

1. Take affirmative action—you're ready.
2. Deliberately program your mind.
3. Remember that the expanded mind never returns to its former shape.
4. Begin your programming with imagination.
5. Know that your mind will affect your body.
6. Believe in what you are telling yourself.
7. Programming your subconscious is a matter of hypnotism.
8. Learn to dehypnotize and rehypnotize yourself.

9. Look at your problems as a deviation from an objective.
10. Get rid of bad attitudes by getting rid of bad behavior.
11. Change physically.
12. Get your forward momentum going by persisting in the direction of your goal; don't let backward momentum push you into failure.
13. Don't worry about people thinking you are not "wrapped too tight."
14. Remember the Kathryn Hulme story and that big goals are possible.
15. Remember how to make the grass grow greener—cut down the weeds and, if necessary, replace them with good grass seed.
16. Establish your own mind power to success reading program.
17. Use modern day technology to accelerate your learning process.
18. Make sure you are now in action.

CHAPTER
7
REJOICE IN FAILURE

I've probably failed at more things than most people have tried, but I certainly don't think I am a failure. Here's an example of a failure: The person who goes through life taking no risks, never changing opportunity into reality, never unleashing his talents to achieve dreamed-of goals—that person has failed to do what he could have done and to become what he could have become.

I've been asked, "Bill, how does it feel to accomplish all you have set out to do?" I have to look over my shoulder to see if the person is talking to someone else. I'll never have an answer to that question because I'll never accomplish all that I can in this lifetime. Even if all of the goals I can imagine were met, I can't see a time when new ones would not be set to replace the old. If that condition ever occurred, I would label it "premature rigor mortis" for surely I would be dead, all would be final and complete. I would merely be awaiting burial.

Life is striving. Living is accomplishing, involvement in one project after another, working toward a goal, achieving and setting your sights on new horizons.

Failure, then, is the opposite of this acting to accomplish. It is the stagnation of maintaining the status quo, the trap of adhering to security, the depression of routine, the death of repetitive living that brings a tomorrow which is the same as yesterday. It's failure that results from doing nothing about life's opportunities rather than doing something about the challenges existing with every dawn of a new day.

Yes, I've failed at more things than most people have tried. I like it that way. In the face of my failures, though, I feel like a roaring success. Here's why: **I would rather fail trying to do something than succeed at doing nothing at all!**

EDISON WAS A FAILURE, WASN'T HE?

Thomas Edison was interviewed by a newspaper reporter shortly after he succeeded in getting his light bulb to burn more than one hundred hours. The reporter, knowing that Edison had tried more than ten thousand different filaments for his experimental bulb, asked Edison how it felt to fail ten thousand times. "I didn't fail ten thousand times," Edison replied. "I found ten thousand ways that will not work."

Of course Edison was right. He had not failed. He succeeded after trying more than ten thousand ways that would not work and his success brought light to the world. I feel the same way as I try thousands of ways that don't work. I'm telling you that I fail, and further, I'm encouraging you to go out and do the same. If you've set your goal-finder, if you're trying, if you're going after opportunity, you will experience some failure along the way. Each failure, how-

EDISON HAD FOUND 10,000 WAYS THAT
WOULD NOT WORK AND HIS SUCCESS
BROUGHT LIGHT TO THE WORLD.

ever, will bring you closer to your goal, so rejoice—you **are** getting closer!

Suppose Edison had quit after ten tries. Suppose he had quit after fifty tries. What if he had said 1,000 attempts are enough? Any reasonable man would have forgiven him if he had quit after his 5,000th or 8,000th attempt or even after experiment 9,999. But then he would have failed.

As long as Edison pursued his objective, held his goal firmly in his mind and worked toward it, he did not have a failure. He was only finding ways that did not work. He could only have failed if at any point he had given up. As long as he continued, he was stalking success.

Your life is the same way. As long as you are striving, as long as you are working toward a goal, as long as you are involved in projects to convert today's opportunities into tomorrow's realities, as long as you are using your mind power to forge ahead, **you cannot fail**! You will find ways that won't work and, more important, you will find those that **do** and will eventually accumulate one success after another.

NEVER CONFUSE PROJECT FAILURE WITH LIFE FAILURE

In the process of accumulating your successes and adding victories to your list, you're going to expect things to happen that won't. You will project results that won't come about. You will wait for realities that won't materialize. You will anticipate other people's help and be kept waiting. You will feel the disappointment of a project failure.

It's during these times that you will be most discouraged. It's at the point of project failure that you will be tempted to quit your mind power to success program and settle for the stagnation of status quo living and become, once again, a victim of the changing world around you rather than being a vital **agent** of that change. When you experience project failure you are at your most vulnerable and your goal seems impossible to reach. You lose focus, your energy seems to leave and self-doubt takes hold.

Stop! This is temporary; the mere fact that the project has failed simply means **it's over**. Get it behind you and move on to the next attempt as you continue your mind power program. The project failure is not a life failure. It is now no longer important and only shows you a way that will not work. You will not make the same mistakes in the future. You will do it differently next time. You will get help where you need it. You will have added to your storehouse of knowledge and have programmed your subconscious to avoid handling this project the same way in future attempts. Failure is merely a part of the autogoal-finding mechanism inside you. With each project failure your focus on the ultimate goal should become sharper. Another obstacle to your getting there has been removed and you are now closer than ever! That's good news!

USE FAILURE TIME TO REINFORCE YOURSELF

You wouldn't be experiencing failure if you were not actively involved in trying to accomplish something—to achieve a goal. So when these occasional setbacks occur, use that opportunity to bolster yourself. Take time to reinforce just what it is you are on your way to accomplishing and take inventory of yourself, your talents and abilities, remembering that in spite of a temporary project failure, you are 100 percent complete, as whole a person as you were before.

Just as fine steel is made even better through the tempering process of heating the metal to make it strong and hard, so you will be made stronger and better able to overcome future obstacles by surviving the test of temporary setbacks.

Here are several points to consider at this time of project failure:

1. **Look at your original plan.** Are your goals still the same? How does the recent situation affect your overall plan? Consider alternative methods of achieving the same results. In most cases you will find that the minor project failure really does not change your goal and that the importance of the situation suddenly diminishes.

2. **Analyze what happened.** Try to see if there is value in the situation as "lesson to be learned." You have probably heard the expression, "Those who do not study history are destined to repeat it." This is the same with those of us who do not analyze what we do wrong on our way to success.

3. **Don't repeat past mistakes.** You must analyze what went wrong and allow proper precautionary signals to become im-

planted in your subconscious to serve as biofeedback warning information if you ever approach a situation where you might repeat the error. However, don't dwell on these negatives. Analyze enough to understand and then leave it. You really want to be looking at these project failures as problems that must be solved in order for you to move on. This means you must become a problem manager as a mind power worker instead of having your problems manage you. Don't stop your overall mind power program during this analysis process. Many big opportunities don't last long enough and they can be missed while you are preoccupied with the problem solving aspect of a brief project failure. Be sure to continue other phases of your program as you treat the problem of the failed program segment.

4. **Believe that all problems can and will be solved.** That is essential. If problems exist but unusual opportunities are also presenting themselves, take the opportunity and trust that you will be able to find solutions to the problems later. You will find that as you take this approach, there is a solution to every problem. You will learn that project failures are offset by compensating victories, but you never find the solutions or achieve the successes if you allow temporary setbacks to stall you. Stalling will only cause anxieties and anxious feelings kill creative thought. You'll need creative thinking to solve the problems and change your failures into victories. Push on. Go forward. Problems are inevitable, but put in their proper perspective they can be one of your best stimulators for success as they move you closer to ways that **do** work.

   As you manage your problems and failures you must do something else that might seem very difficult—**maintain your sense of humor.** Purposely look for some humor in the situation. Find one aspect of your circumstance that is laughable and dwell on that part for a time. By doing so you take the sting out of the situation.

5. **Establish a new plan to offset the failure.** Now you need a compensating victory. How trite it sounds, but I believe, "If you don't succeed at first, try, try, again." Now that you have analyzed the failure and have found the cause, you can try again, but this time with a modified approach. You can eliminate the errors and push forward with a new method or at least with further insight, with a sharpened awareness and even with a

PAST FAILURES CAN BE TURNED INTO FUTURE SUCCESSES. USE FAILURES AS LEARNING EXPERIENCES.

caution that will greatly reduce the percentage chance of failure. Your new plan will certainly be superior to the first because it has the benefit of a failure to help you develop it. You are now better equipped to use your intelligence, guided by your experience.

6. **Take a close look at yourself.** Self-esteem building time. Take an emotional/logical self-appraisal vitamin pill. What would you do about a person who constantly shoots you down? How would you respond to someone who tells you your best ideas are dumb, that your temporary project failure is only natural because it was destined to be a failure from the start? Would you allow it? Would you keep that person around? Would you dispute the comments? Would you let someone constantly put you down? You say you wouldn't? Are you sure? Who puts you down more than any other person at times of project failure? **You do!** That's right, you do a good job of it and the put-downs that come from ourselves are the most devastating of all. These put-downs come from the center of our existence. They are driven by emotion and what seems to be logic. When this happens you completely paralyze your mind power to success mechanism. You stifle your creativity. Here are a few points to consider as you put yourself back on the track:

a. **Be a cheerleader.** Listen to your good ideas. Compliment yourself on everything that you have done right so far. Take a look back and remember where you were before you started your program. Imagine where you will be a year from now. Visualize great victories. Congratulate yourself for being a mind power worker and for sticking to your program even when things don't always go right. Think about all of the opportunities that still exist and imagine them becoming wonderful new realities.

b. **Appraise your competition accurately.** Don't let competition get to you. Don't let competitive situations wear you down. Use competition as one of the most constructive forces in your mind power program by making your primary competition none other than yourself. Set your own standards, then compete to beat yourself at your own game. Under these circumstances who wins if you lose? Of course, **you do!** In this way, failure will become the benchmark of success.

THERE ARE A FEW HURDLES TO
OVERCOME AS YOU PUT YOURSELF
BACK ON THE TRACK.

c. **Be forgiving of yourself.** Be your own best friend. You are going to make mistakes that will lead to failures. The worst thing you can do is mentally beat yourself for your mistakes. Remember, every day is a new beginning if you can put all of yesterday's regrets behind you and move into a tomorrow of new opportunities, another 86,400 seconds to invest in your mind power to success program. Never say, "I wish I had done this or that"; instead, look at your mistakes and say, "The next time, **I will do it!**"

d. **Be bold enough to practice self-love.** You must practice really loving yourself. Think of all of the victories that you've had in the past and think about all of the reasons you are a special person. Love yourself for all of these thoughts. You cannot become truly self-assured and secure until you genuinely love yourself. Look at all of the great people you have heard about or have known and see how confident and relaxed they are. They project a relaxed manner while at the same time exude sincere humility. How can this be? It's simple. You can love yourself and still be humble by realizing that true humility is never thinking less of yourself but is a matter of thinking more of those around you. So love yourself and the rest of the world, too.

SOME MAGNIFICENT FAILURES

When I began this chapter I said that I'd probably failed at more things than others have tried. Taking my own advice, I refuse to dwell on those failures, but I'd like to list a few here and show you how they are handled to become victories instead of stumbling blocks when they were turned inside out.

I THOUGHT I WAS A HOTSHOT PILOT

During my army days, I fantasized about becoming an army helicopter pilot. I sought the opportunity of going to flight school and applied and took a check flight with a pilot to make sure that I would truly enjoy being in a light observation helicopter. That first ride was fantastic! I still remember the thrill of it. I remember flying over Pittsburgh and feeling as if I were on a Ferris wheel five thousand feet in the air. A small helicopter is much different from a fixed wing

I THOUGHT I WAS A HOTSHOT HELICOPTER PILOT. I ENDED UP MAKING LEMONADE OUT OF A LEMON.

airplane since you are able to look out the front, the sides, the top and even see down to the ground between your feet. I knew then that I had to become a helicopter pilot. I even decided that I would reenlist in the army and risk having to spend three more years after flight school. To my way of thinking, it was worth it.

I went through officer's training without any problem. We were then sent to flight school and I was a real whiz. I was the first to solo in my class. But suddenly something happened that turned everything around. When it came time for my check flight, I failed. I was given another check flight and again I failed. In my eagerness to succeed, I had developed many bad flying habits that were sloppy and I could not unlearn these habits fast enough in order to please the check pilot. I was a very good seat-of-the-pants pilot, but I wasn't flying the army way. I realized that my subconscious mind had been programmed with a technique of flying that wouldn't allow me to complete the course of instruction. The army didn't have time to retrain me and I was washed out of the program. What a disappointment! Imagine, I had reenlisted for three years and now my goal was unattainable. I felt that I had really failed at life. I can remember being so upset that I was physically ill. I had such an emotional reaction that my body began to void itself of food and water in a way that I had never felt before. I had chills, stomach cramps and was sure that some dreaded disease had attacked me. I even went to the emergency room of the base hospital. They simply gave me a sedative and allowed me to adjust to the trauma of a very upsetting failure. From Texas I was sent to Germany as an enlisted man and it was there that I became a public relations specialist.

Remember the story about my writing to Kathryn Hulme? While I was in Germany, after my failure to become a helicopter pilot, I found a wonderful new opportunity. It was for the work I did as a public relations specialist that I was finally awarded the Army Commendation Medal for having the best newspaper in the Army, Navy, Air Force and Marine Corps.

From this failure to become a helicopter pilot and an officer in the army I learned three things:
1. It was important to continue to believe in myself.
2. I would not let that single project failure become a life failure.
3. I took a "lemon" of a circumstance—the fact that I had to finish my service term—and made some good lemonade from it.

HOW I LOST MY RADIO JOB

Not all successes are necessarily stepping stones to another success if they're not handled properly. In Chapter 3, I explained that even at age sixteen I was always looking for unusual opportunities. At that time I was a radio announcer. I want to tell you how I lost that job because it represents another failure and another lesson.

During the time that I was a teenage radio announcer, so many other successes followed that I began to think I was indispensable. One day the station manager walked in and introduced me to a new man whom he said would be temporarily replacing me on the "Night Shift" program for the summer. He indicated that I would continue to be employed, but he wanted me to switch to days. Well, this certainly did not fit in with my desire to be talking to teenage girls from eight o'clock until midnight. I couldn't understand why the change was being made. Then I found out that the new man was the boss's nephew and that he needed a job for the summer. He could only work nights and, therefore, he got the best spot. I marched into the boss's office and told him that if this happened I was going to quit immediately. He said, "Okay." That's how I failed to hold my job and progress in the world of radio broadcasting which could have eventually led to a career of television newscasting, which could have eventually... but, that's all past supposition.

I LEARNED WE SHOULD NEVER GIVE BOSSES ULTIMATUMS. USE A PRESENT POSITION TO BUILD TO SOMETHING BETTER.

There was something to be learned from this little episode which resulted in failure:

1. Never give your boss an ultimatum. He always has the power and when you give him an ultimatum, you give him no choice. I learned that I should have seen the situation as a problem and worked to overcome and change it to my advantage. I could have gotten experience on the day shift and been a more valuable man because I would have been capable of handling additional programming.

2. An opportunity to take a small talent and build it into a bigger one was missed because I was reacting to emotion rather than applying logic.

3. Situations such as this stay with you forever. For this reason, I know that I will not make the same mistake again. I will work it out instead of working it up.

I FAILED TO MAKE THE TEAM

I wanted to be on the football team in the worst way. I tried and I tried, but I was a terrible football player. I wasn't coordinated enough to catch the ball. I couldn't throw accurately. I didn't have enough weight for a lineman—I was a miserable failure. Still, I didn't want to be left out of the football game, so I looked for a way that I could be part of it. Eventually I did a terrific job as a stadium announcer. What did I learn from this failure?

1. Project failures are not life failures. It was a matter of **changing the project into a problem.**
2. I had to manage the problem and not have the problem manage me.
3. By looking for another solution I accomplished my objective. I was part of every football game both at home and as a spotter at the away games.

I FAILED TO MAKE THE TEAM BUT BEING A STADIUM ANNOUNCER WASN'T ALL BAD. I LEARNED TO CHANGE THE PROJECT INTO A PROBLEM AND LOOK FOR ANOTHER SOLUTION.

I could go on and on, describing the many failures that I've had during my forty-two years. I could also show you ways in which these failures have strengthened me and have led to success after success. I do think, however, having read this far, that you get the point. I would rather that you now think of your failures, figure out how you can handle them as mere problems and manage those problems for eventual successes instead of having the problems handle you.

Be sure that as you work on your mind power to success program you expect some failures to occur and be ready to overcome them. Don't let them bring you down. Remember that failures bring you closer to your successes as you find ways that will not work. Rejoice in failures because you are able to use them as the strength giving, tempering, character building aspects of becoming what you are meant to be.

POINTS TO REMEMBER

1. Stay busy pursuing your goal; successful people generally fail at more things than others even try.
2. Failure is the opposite of activity, the stagnation of maintaining the status quo.
3. Don't fall into the trap of adhering to security.
4. Develop the philosophy that you would rather fail trying to do something great than succeed at doing nothing at all.
5. Edison didn't fail more than ten thousand times; he found ten thousand ways that would not work as he went on to give the world the light bulb.
6. Never confuse your project failures with life failures—use them as growing experiences.
7. Use your failure time to reinforce yourself.
8. Look at the original plan of action.
9. Analyze what happened.
10. Establish a new plan to offset your project failure.
11. Take a close look at yourself and be a cheerleader.
12. Appraise your competition accurately.
13. Be forgiving of yourself.
14. Be bold enough to practice self-love.

15. As you work your mind power to success program, expect some failure.
16. Remember that failures bring you closer to your successes as you find ways that will not work.
17. Rejoice in failures because you are able to use them as strengths.

CHAPTER
8
HABITS RUN YOU

In order to release mind power to success for the future, you will have to liberate yourself from slavery. The slavery I'm talking about has nothing to do with the bondage into which another person would put you. It has to do with the slavery that results from taking on a powerful master. That master is **habit.**

As long as you are a slave to bad habits, you cannot achieve mind power to success, you cannot energize your autogoal-finder to seek new goals, you cannot be an agent of change. As long as you continue to do the things that you feel **compelled** to do, you will not be able to do the things you now feel you **want** to do. Think about those words for a minute. Think about one habit that you have. You'll know because you're compelled to respond to that habit; you don't have total control over your mind or life. Without total control over your mind and your life, you will be unable to use the mind power within you.

These statements are rather strong and, at this point, you might feel that I'm bordering on being intrusive and offensive. You must understand, however, that I, too, had many bad habits that needed to be changed, eliminated or controlled before I could make further progress. In this chapter I will discuss habits that nearly stopped me from making a career change to break away from the field of mediocrity, do what I wanted to do, become what I wanted to become and have what I wanted to have.

YOU CAN'T POSSIBLY ACHIEVE MIND POWER TO SUCCESS IF YOU ARE A SLAVE TO HABIT.

The methods in this chapter and Chapter 9 for controlling or changing habits have been tried and proven. They are reported here so that you can take advantage of what has been successful in the past, condense your own program of improvement and move closer to the realization of your individual, personal goals.

GET FULL CONTROL OF YOUR MIND

You now know how your mind works. It's time to get full control of it as you take charge of your habitual reactions to everyday situations. Psychologists tell us that we really control only about 5 percent of our daily activities. The other 95 percent of those activities are basically routine, dictated to us by other people and circumstances. We merely react to these people and circumstances in the same way, each and every day, developing habit patterns that carry us through from dawn to dusk.

Here's something you must understand: You are not a body with a mind as you have been taught all your life. You've heard the reference to "a healthy mind in a healthy body." That statement, quoted periodically throughout your life, has simply reinforced a falsehood. In truth, **you are really a mind with a body.**

Look at the people around you. Even though we talk about the uniqueness of the individual, you will notice that all of these people are physically similar. The difference between one person and another is not the physical presence, not the body; we are all composed of the same chemicals in nearly the same mix. In order to live, all of us must breathe, must have meals every day, must get a certain amount of rest and exercise to maintain our health. As you look at other individuals, you can very clearly see that, under normal circumstances, we are endowed with the same physical capabilities. The only **real** difference between you and the other person is the difference that exists between your ears; that is, it's the difference that exists in your mind compared to what exists in the minds of others.

Dwell on that thought. Combine it with the fact that 95 percent of your life is controlled by your habits and you see the importance of habit control. To say it another way, the difference between you and another person is the difference that comes from your having more control over your mind and its power than the individual who has given his mind power to the master of habits who has enslaved him. "Master" does not necessarily have to mean some fictitious, misty concept—it can mean a specific individual or set of circumstances in a particular life. I'm talking about the facts and realities of the things that are currently controlling you.

YOU KEEP ON KIDDING YOURSELF

Up to this point, as you read the message of this book, you may have been trying to do everything asked of you at the end of the chapters. That's the way it should be. As you go through these exercises, you're gaining mind power to success. You're on your way to becoming the individual you want to be. You're getting closer to having what you want to have. You have certainly begun to change. You might also have found, as indicated in Chapter 7 on failures, that you are not achieving success as quickly as you had originally expected. Don't be discouraged. You just might be impatient. I hope so. In fact, I expect it because out of your impatience will come a drive to succeed.

Your lack of progress might be, however, a matter of your still being the slave to habits that are dictating 95 percent of your daily activities. It could be that your habits are holding you back, as if you had a ball and chain attached to your leg. Up to this point, you could be kidding yourself.

Let me explain. When you think of your habits, like many people, you will make a conscious effort to do something about them. This is usually done on a large scale at the beginning of each year. Yes, hundreds of thousands of New Year's resolutions are made because people generally recognize their bad habits and usually want to change or eliminate them. For a period of time, you and I and others actually carry out the resolve to change.

Take a moment to reflect on the times that you have made New Year's resolutions. It's like the fellow who said he could quit smoking any time; he knew it was true because he had already quit nine times. How long did you carry out your resolutions? Did you find that the result of making them was just a matter of kidding yourself?

There is a great deal of difference in promising yourself you are going to do something and in making a promise to another individual. When you make a promise to someone else, you usually move into action to make sure it's kept. When you make a promise to yourself, you may or may not act on it. You **kid yourself** about your intentions. You break more promises to yourself than you do to other people. The danger in this is that **if you don't move into action, you really will not be able to modify or change your behavior;** therefore, you will not be able to change a habit.

When you break a promise to yourself you have the importance of the situation backward. You must live with yourself every day and, therefore, must realize that the conscience mechanism inside you reacts the same when you break a promise to yourself as when you break a promise to another individual. So breaking a promise to yourself will evoke guilt feelings deep down inside. If you are one of those people who constantly makes but then breaks promises to yourself, you must realize your habit is slowing down your mind power to success program. Now it's time to be really truthful with yourself—one of the hardest things you have to do.

MAKE ONLY ONE PROMISE

When I found myself constantly breaking promises to myself, I discovered a way to break that bad habit. I decided that I had to discipline myself to **keep only one promise:** I promised myself **never to break a promise to myself.**

With this rule, I began to make progress. I made sure that whatever I promised myself was something that I really was able to attain. I also adjusted my goals so that they were attractive, but not unreasonable, to have accomplished within a certain period of time. I became a better planner. I carefully analyzed situations before I made myself any promises.

As you can well imagine, this takes a tremendous amount of will power. But isn't that what this book is about? **Will power is mind power.** Once you have set your direction, once you have made a promise to yourself, many things will come up that will make it difficult, if not nearly impossible, to keep your promise. Often the situations that arise will force you to decide between keeping your promise and doing something for another individual. These are the most difficult circumstances. For example, I made a promise to allow so many hours each day for self-development over a period of six months. During that six-month program, many people demanded more of my time and imposed on the self-development promise I'd made. It was necessary for me to appear almost selfish in my attempt to make sure that I carried out my program and kept my promise to myself.

The people you disappoint could be as close as a spouse, a parent, a child or a brother. In my case it was a brother who couldn't understand how necessary it was for me to complete my individual task.

Throughout the six-month period I often had to explain over and over that I was unable to participate in one activity or another because I had promised myself that time. Since this is such an unusual concept and such a deviation from the way people generally conduct their lives, it was nearly incomprehensible to those who heard my explanation. In some cases, because it was impossible to do anything else, I had to tell a white lie to more logically explain reasons for not being able to go somewhere or participate in an activity.

As you continue to develop your mind power, as you strive to become different, as you rise above the field of mediocrity, other people will see your activities as strange. You will be breaking away from the norm. This is only natural as you evolve into a new individual. **Remember, the difference between you and the other person as you acquire and use mind power is the difference that exists in your mind.** As you change, those differences are going to be noticed, but they will not necessarily be understood. You cannot, however, allow negative feedback from other people to stop you from making progress. You must gain control of more than 5 percent of your life so that you can change. All the while that my friends, brother and other family members pressured me in subtle ways to remain the same, I insisted on keeping my promise to myself. From that first six-month period of discipline, I developed a wonderful **new habit**. Today, that habit has also become a **master**. The habit I developed was: **keeping the promises I made to myself.** From that point on, it was a matter of looking at my negative habits and knocking them off, one by one.

The first thing I had to look at was smoking cigarettes. This was certainly a negative habit. As we will learn later, this habit was also a destructive reaction to stress. I had to start with a promise to myself that I was going to stop. Since I already had practice keeping promises to myself, a pattern had been established and I successfully accomplished the mission.

I became liberated from several other habits. I concentrated on them one at a time and allowed approximately a month for conquering each one. In this way, I became freer and freer each month. Remember from our chapters on how the mind works: It takes approximately twenty-one days to a month to change an activity or to have an activity properly programmed into the subconscious mind. For that reason, as I tried to break negative habits, I made sure that I allowed myself sufficient time to be successful.

How about you? Have you said to yourself, "Tomorrow I'm **really** going to start on my program"? Have you promised yourself that you are going to finish a job that has been waiting for your attention for a long time? Have you looked at yourself and said that you're not what you want to be or not headed where you want to be going? Have you decided that smoking is bad for you? Have you thought that you might be overweight? Have you known for a long time that your daily activities are habitual and nonproductive? Have you found that you've been making promises to yourself and then breaking them? Are you trying to justify your habits after giving up trying to break them? Are you saying to yourself that you smoke two packs of cigarettes a day because they actually relax you? Are you saying that if you didn't smoke you would probably gain weight? Are you telling yourself that alcohol calms you down, that it does just as good a job in the morning and the afternoon as it does in the evening? Are you throwing away your time every day on worthless activity and not allowing development time because that's the way you've been most of your life? These are all habits that you can and will break. You will be able to master your habits and not allow them to keep you perpetually chained, retarding your progress in your mind power to success program.

Mark Twain said, "A habit cannot be tossed out the window; it must be coaxed down the stairs one step at a time." Habits which are unchecked are really cobwebs in the mind that change to cables. If your habits are not resisted, they very quickly become necessities.

"A HABIT CANNOT BE TOSSED OUT THE WINDOW; IT MUST BE COAXED DOWN THE STAIRS ONE STEP AT A TIME."

OLD HABITS ARE LIKE NAIL HOLES

Once you've broken a habit you have the advantage of a little reminder that will stay with you for the rest of your life. This reminder is not necessarily negative, but it does point out the nature of a habit because it has a tendency to leave a mark for a lifetime. Once upon a time there was a father who, in guiding his son, told him to drive a nail into a fence post every time he did something bad and to withdraw one nail each time he did something good. The boy did exactly as his father requested, but he regretted that he was not able to get rid of the nail holes that were left. This is the same way with the record of our lives. We may change our program, we can turn over a new leaf, but we will always have a reminder of our former flaws. Habits that are continued for a long time become very hard to break. Even after they're broken their "nail holes" stay and remind us of our former bad decisions.

For this reason, we want to be sure from this point on that we monitor our lives in such a way that the habits formed are those that are good, beneficial, day-to-day reactions to life's situations.

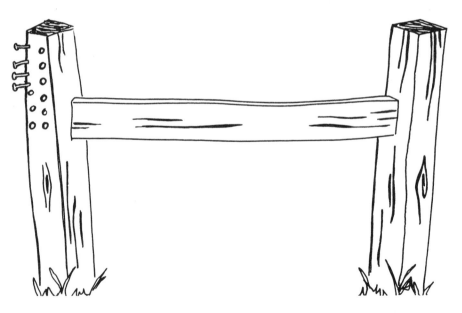

OLD HABITS ARE LIKE NAIL HOLES IN A FENCE POST—ONCE THE NAILS ARE REMOVED, THERE'S A MARK LEFT FOR A LIFETIME.

YOUR HABITS INDICATE WHAT
YOU THINK OF YOURSELF

Spend the rest of the day or all day tomorrow observing what people do. You will notice that how a person habitually acts reveals what he thinks of himself. Things that people do as a matter of habit come from the core of their existence. If other people act this way, you can be sure that you and I also react the same when it comes to the habit reflecting how we feel about ourselves.

The way you act will let the world know what you think of yourself. Your habits are just like the clothes you wear. You have heard that clothes make the man; well, habits make the person in much the same way. We all "wear" habits because they fit us; in most cases, habits fit us like a glove. They are truly a reflection of how we see ourselves from the inside out.

When you develop a program of changing your habits, you will automatically be changing how you think about yourself and will eventually become the new person that you see. Since habits are worn like clothing, others are also going to see the new person and say that they have a new friend.

ONLY 5 PERCENT OF YOU IS
CONSCIOUSLY CONTROLLED

It is worth restating that psychologists tell us about 95 percent of all of our activity is controlled by our habits. Keep thinking about that as you develop a program for changing your habits. Aren't most of your activities routine and habit controlled? Don't you do the same things day after day with very little change? Don't you react in much the same way to similar circumstances every time? Of course you do. You drive to work the same way in the morning. Prior to even going to work, you probably set the alarm clock for the same time. Breakfast may not have been exactly the same as the day before, but it was probably similar and took the same amount of time to prepare it and eat. Sitting at your desk at work, getting into position on the assembly line or punching in was the same today as it was yesterday. This isn't **all** wrong. We need the stability and comfort of daily security which comes from repeated actions. However, in our mind power to success program, we must analyze how many of these activities are actually bad habits that keep us from positive change.

I KNEW WHERE THE BATHROOMS WERE

In the hallway of our office building one afternoon, a friend asked me why I didn't change jobs and companies long before I actually had to become a private consultant. The friend knew that I inwardly had a desire to be on my own. At that time, though, I really didn't have an answer. Upon reflection, I knew that I could increase my income, that I could have more time for myself and Kathy, that I would be able to do some varied and interesting things. I also knew I would prefer being independent, and I knew I would grow. Still, I clung to the old, familiar, usual routine that was comfortable and secure.

My friend said, "I know why you don't make the change. It's because you know where the bathrooms are." I suppose that was right. I was comfortable in familiar surroundings. I was secure within my habitualized living—I knew where the rest rooms were.

The comment from my friend became a thought seed that caused another change in my life. I started to think about the direction that I wanted to go and started to change my daily habits. My entire pattern was altered as I began to move in a new direction and prepared for a career change.

Perhaps this is where you are now. Maybe you picked up this book because you are at a crossroads in your life or career. This chapter can be most beneficial to you because it can be the starting point of the changes that must be made so you can make the big change in your life. Since 95 percent of your activities are controlled by habit you must begin changing them now.

THINK OF YOUR HABIT AS A REACTION

Simply put, your habits are reactions to every situation that occurs, reactions you've learned to perform without having to think. Smoking a cigarette when you're nervous is a negative reaction to stress. Overeating is often the same. In order for you to change the habit you must change the reaction to something that will benefit you. Habits are automatic responses to situations and can be positive instead of negative. Consider the following example:

When my daughter was very young, she decided that she wanted to learn to play the organ. I went to the music store and bought an organ that had just about every geegaw imaginable. Of course I expected Stacy to "grow into" the instrument. In fact, the salesman assured me that this would happen.

The organ was delivered and Stacy began her lessons. After one week of lessons, I asked her to play for me. She played, but it was not music. The sounds she produced were more like noise than anything else. My next purchase was a set of headphones for her that plugged into the organ and blocked the sound coming from the instrument. I didn't listen to her practicing anymore, either.

After a month I asked her if she could play one short tune. She unplugged the earphones and allowed the organ to produce sounds as loud as she wanted them. What a remarkable difference! Stacy was producing music. I don't think I've ever heard anyone play "Largo" any better since then, although my appraisal could be colored by the relationship. But my point regarding habits is: Whether good or bad, habits are acquired the same way you acquire any activity that you do well—by repeating actions that eventually saturate your subconscious.

Another example comes from the year I was sixteen and decided to buy a vehicle that would allow me to carry all of my magic equipment. This meant that it either had to be a truck or large automobile. I settled for an old hearse. I painted it with pictures of rabbits coming out of a hat and had a traveling show. Of course I didn't travel far since this was yet another activity along with school and the three jobs that I had in Ellwood City. Still, the vehicle gave me mobility to do children's birthday parties, women's clubs, Rotary clubs, etc.

My father wanted to make sure that I developed good driving habits. He decided he was going to teach me to drive the right way. He took me to Ewing Park, a small park just outside of Ellwood City where most youngsters learned to drive. I remember very distinctly his having me go halfway up a hill, pushing in the clutch, putting on the brake and taking the vehicle out of gear. At that point he said, "Bill, I want you to continue up the hill, but you cannot drift back one inch."

That was cruel! The vehicle didn't have an automatic transmission, the gearshift was on the floor. I had to push in the clutch, skip my foot from the brake to the gas pedal while at the same time releasing the hand brake, shifting into low gear, adjusting the clutch to the engine speed—it was absolutely impossible. I was trying to do the whole thing consciously without having developed any habits. I would have been a threat to anybody on the highway if I had tried to drive that vehicle that day in traffic. Naturally, after I'd practiced that maneuver and several others, I learned to drive the hearse.

The point is, when we are trying to develop good habits, we must practice them over and over until they become part of us. No matter how difficult the activity may seem at first, it's this continual practice that's going to put the activity into our subconscious mind and enable us to do it automatically. It's the same way with bad habits. We break bad habits by not doing them or by replacing them with a good habit. Yes, it can be done.

Good habits are acquired slowly and deliberately through practice. Bad habits are eliminated in the same way. **Do not** mistake habits for addictions. Bad habits can be broken and new habits can be established without symptoms of withdrawal, but stopping an addiction causes withdrawal symptoms. This chapter is not addressing that particular problem. I'm only talking about changing your habits, making a conscious decision to do so. You must act out the new habit that is going to replace your bad one. The musician can learn new songs; he doesn't have to stay with only the songs he has played in the past. You, too, can learn to produce beautiful new music when you learn to conquer your bad habits and replace them with good ones.

LEARNING TO DRIVE AN AUTOMOBILE IS A MATTER OF FORMING A HABIT IN THE SUBCONSCIOUS MIND.

Changing habits, like all mind power principles in this book, is not really that difficult. It begins with a decision. You must decide to change. It's as easy as deciding to drive to work a different way each morning. You just do it, repeat, then do it again, and soon you've established a new pattern. Then your behavior adjusts your attitude, your attitude gives you a new way of life and your life-style gives you a new destiny.

WHAT ARE YOU GOING TO DO NOW?

Throughout this discussion I hope that you have been doing some self-appraising. While you did your self-appraisal, I'm going to assume that you mentally lifted some habits that you know you must break, those that must be replaced with new ones to speed you on your way rather than retard your progress. Now you must stop and reconsider some questions from Chapter 1: Do you really want to change? Do you really want to discover all that's special to you? Do you want to focus your talents and abilities? Do you want to be on fire with success? Do you want the world to watch? Do you **really?** That's just great! Now you'll find out how you can harness those habits and make them work for you.

POINTS TO REMEMBER

1. To release mind power to success you must liberate yourself from habit slavery.
2. Get full control of your mind by taking control of your habitual reactions to everyday situations.
3. Psychologists tell us that we really control only about 5 percent of our daily activities.
4. You are really a mind with a body.
5. The difference between you and anybody else lies between your ears.
6. Stop kidding yourself and don't make promises to yourself that you do not keep.
7. To get rid of a habit you must coax it down the stairs one step at a time.

8. Old habits are like nail holes in a fence post; even after you have removed the nails, they leave a mark forever.
9. Your habits indicate what you think of yourself.
10. Think of your habit as a reaction to a situation.
11. Good habits are acquired slowly and deliberately through practice; bad habits are gotten rid of the same way.

CHAPTER

9

HARNESS
YOUR HABITS

Have you ever been pushed around by another person or manipulated by the circumstances of your life? Do you yield to the demands of the day, no matter what happens? Do you allow yourself to drift?

I once reacted in much the same way, drifting, allowing myself to be controlled by others or my environment. People are programmed this way. You've heard the clichés time after time:

"What are you gonna do?"

"That's the way it is."

"You can't fight city hall."

"It's just meant to be."

Nonsense! You can change and you will. You can control your life and your environment and you'll do it with the mind power that comes from controlling habits that ultimately determine your destiny. You **can** and **will** harness your habits and make them a positive, driving force in your life. You will learn and practice **fight** instead of **flight** and develop an aggressive attitude that helps you say, "I am important to myself and to all those around me who touch my life."

When you've done this, a new energy is released from within you that will give you power to do what you want to do, to have what you desire and to become what you want to be. Only after you've developed an aggressive attitude toward your mind power program can you overcome all of the obstacles that are going to be put in your way. You're going to find that dedication to your purpose will set you apart from others and even cause conflicts in your life. You must develop the good habits that are required of the individual who is committed to a direction. These good habits will automatically keep you on course and turn away others who would interfere.

I TOLD MY BOSS "NO"

There was a time when my superior at the company where I'd worked for fifteen years came to me and said he was upset about my lecturing, writing and participating in outside activities. He indicated that he was sure these activities must take much of my thinking time, time that should be devoted to the company. He lectured me on how an executive is paid to be part of the company twenty-four hours a day. He demanded that I immediately stop all activities not related directly to the company.

My additional activities were never carried out at the expense of the company or by using its resources. The company often benefited from the notoriety I was achieving in the industry through increased orders and my ability to get appointments with even the most aloof prospects as a result of being on the platform for many convention programs. When the boss said, "Be a good employee, Bill," to me it meant, "You're getting too much notice and I don't like it." The boss really had a problem.

This is not an unusual situation. Many negatives in the form of authority or just as a force of everyday living are going to threaten your mind power program as you develop and grow. For this reason you **must** cultivate the habit of reacting forcefully and aggressively.

In response to my boss's request I told him, "I have no intention of stopping my outside activities. Absolutely not. In fact, I have every intention of increasing this part of my life and the company will be the loser if you don't want to participate." Those were firing words. This boss went to the president and demanded my head for insubordination. However, the president wouldn't have been the president if he hadn't been a much wiser man than my boss. He told my boss to leave me alone. That year at work was not a pleasant one, but it was a tremendous growth time.

Aggressive behavior in the direction of your goals quickly becomes a habit that releases great amounts of energy to propel you forward at an accelerated rate. At every resistance, I became stronger. My desire grew, my activities increased, I was twice as productive as I had been and my audiences were more enthusiastic about my talks than they'd ever been before. I became somewhat obnoxious as I habitually pointed out to the boss the many new activities I had taken on and sent him news clippings, testimonial letters and congratulatory remarks from other industry executives, all of whom were his peers or his superiors. This had a wonderful effect on him as far as I was concerned—he quit speaking to me.

I'll not belabor this story. Suffice it to say that now, as an independent with my own consulting company, I make at least twice as much money as he, have more free time and do more of what I want to do when I want to do it than he ever did or ever will. (That last comment may not be true—he could read this book and develop mind power to success. I think I'll send him a copy.)

Use aggression and emotion to reinforce your determination. You may not have a real-life adversary as I did. However, you do have a detractor within yourself. It's this detractor against which you must direct your aggression, against which you must get angry enough to release the kind of energy necessary to propel yourself forward. I would not let the fear of the boss's threat push me backward. I used the situation to drive me forward.

There is a force in you that is wound tightly like a spring, and it's about to be let loose in a controlled yet steadily powerful driving action that will increase your momentum as you get closer to your goals.

DEVELOP CONSCIOUS THOUGHT CONTROL

Now that you have decided that you are going to be assertive, you can become involved in successful habit control. It's going to take a "fighting mad" determination to get involved in a series of habit control techniques that will help get rid of unwanted habits and add habits that will enhance your life.

UNDERSTAND WHAT INFLUENCES YOUR BEHAVIOR

To truly stick to your habit development program, you must be at the center of it. You must make it the core of your existence while initial changes are taking place. Everything you do, all of your thinking, all that you say must contain, in some way, a consciousness of your habit control program. This involves a conscious control of your activities, or behavior. Before we look at specific techniques, you should know how your environment affects you.

LEND ME AN "EAR"

I'm going to ask you to lend an EAR to what will be described next. By EAR I mean:

E = Environment
A = Action
R = Result

You'll see how your **environment** influences you to take **action** that **results** in a particular behavior and eventually becomes a habit.

Things that happen in your everyday world are going to cause you to take certain actions. These actions will eventually affect your behavior in similar circumstances. This behavior will shape your thinking in such a way that the final result will be what you truly believe. Here are a few examples:

Environment: Everyone in my group smokes.
Action: I want to fit in, so I smoke, too.
Result: I have the smoking habit.

Environment: All my friends are A or B students.
Action: I must study hard to keep up.
Result: It's now my habit to set aside two hours a night for my schoolwork.

Environment: My parents drink a lot.
Action: I use booze whenever possible.
Result: I have become an alcoholic.

What you see in the last example is typical of a family situation as it influences a child. That example could be written differently if the child uses conscious habit control, as follows:

Environment: My parents drink a lot.
Action: Their performance turns me off.
Result: I'll never touch the stuff.

The result difference in the above examples concerning alcohol indicates a method of behavior change even though the environmental influence is the same. The second result is a matter of the individual's gaining conscious control of the action and guiding the behavior so that the overall result is a positive direction. Perhaps this pleasant result came about because of additional environmental influences such as this:

Environment: My parents drink a lot.
Action: They get drunk and abusive.
Result: I resent their actions.

YOU MUST LEARN TO DO BATTLE WITH YOUR ENVIRONMENT. IN THIS WAY YOU CAN CHANGE THE RESULTS OF YOUR ACTION. YOU WILL THEN FORM NEW HABITS.

This in turn changes the perception of the environment:

Environment: Abuse of alcohol.
Action: Avoidance of alcohol.
Result: Dislike of alcohol.

One way of influencing the behavioral outcome of a situation is to change the **environment** so it causes a different **action** and turns out a different **result**. How do you do that? To change your actions and have them affect the results, or habits, you must change your environmental influences.

CHANGE YOUR WORLD FROM BAD TO GOOD

To move forward in your mind power program, you must change your environment from bad to good. That statement may sound elementary but the technique is really that basic. To help you focus on what I'm saying, take a moment to play with the EAR concept. If you allow your situation to remain Bad, you are adding a "B" to the formula and getting "BEAR." That's exactly what you'll have—a real BEAR of a time making your mind power program work for you. What happens when you change your environment to Good using the letter "G"? You come up with "GEAR" which means you are now GEARed for success.

This is pretty corny, isn't it? You bet, but it's intended to remind you what often is necessary when you need a change in your life. Look at what is influencing you and adjust those influences so that they have a more positive impact on you.

MENTAL ENVIRONMENTAL CHANGING

Many people have said about me, "Bill lives in his own world." They're right, of course. I don't believe this world is exactly as it should be and I intend to leave it slightly better than it was when I came into it. One way I change it is to first imagine my own environment as I want it to be. This imagined environment causes me to act in a modified way and the result of the way I act is much different than it would have been if I'd merely acted on what really existed.

Sometimes you can't change your physical environment; therefore, it's nearly impossible to GEAR up in a physical way. When this happens you will want to use your mind power to consciously change how you **think** about the situation and actually change the **influence** the situation has on you.

The example of the drinking parent was such a situation. The child adjusted the environment to see the drinking as a negative and rejected it. You must do the same. You must find ways to adjust your so-called "real" world so that you modify the environment. This will enable you to take action against this new mental picture of the world around you.

As you learned in earlier chapters, the subconscious mind cannot tell the difference between the real and the imagined. For this reason you can adjust your input regarding your **environment**, change your **action** and achieve different **results**.

Here's an example of how this mental environmental changing works: In America nearly three-fourths of the people who go through their lives in poverty have the opportunity to take advantage of all benefits offered by the free enterprise system. Yet, they don't. I think this is because they are living in the result of a poverty environment and act out that role as shown:

Environment: Surrounded by poverty.
Action: Thinking and talking about poverty.
Result: Living in poverty.

These people fear poverty so they think poverty and talk poverty until everything they do involves survival action against the poverty they accept as being perpetually real. To gain riches, to rise above poverty, the action must first start with a "wealth consciousness":

Environment: Wealth is possible in this world.
Action: I must find ways to get it.
Result: Searching and working to achieve (habit).

Habit really implies a predisposition to a situation due to repetition of action that keeps bringing the same result.

If you were down to your last few dollars and spent them on this book, I would say you did the right thing merely because of the above example. **Don't accept your world as you see it.** See your world as **you want it to be.** Make a habit of acting on this new mental environment and the result will be wonderful changes in your life. Your autogoal-finder is **not** broken. It will guide you onward and upward.

"But, I'm doing okay," you're saying. "I just want to do better." Fine. Keep lending me your EAR. Put on paper exactly what you want to accomplish. Put it in the form of an environment in the formula. Beneath it write your anticipated action and then put down your expected result. That's easy, isn't it? Now comes the harder part. Get aggressively into action. Get "fighting mad" at yourself. Energize your goal-finder and you will start to develop new habits that will propel you in the right direction.

HABITS ARE RESULTS

It should be no revelation to you that habits are the results of your new actions based on mental or physical environmental changes. In the EAR formula, to develop good, new habits or get rid of bad, old habits, you must control both the environmental influences and the actions you take.

Remember, environmental changes must be accomplished in two ways:

1. Change the environment **physically.**
2. Change the environment **mentally.**

Now on to action change that will give you new results, or new habits.

ACTIONS THAT WILL CHANGE HABITS

Various actions can be taken to change your habits. You have selectivity. Not only can you change habits, but you can also create new ones and completely get rid of the bad ones. Several actions can be easily applied and selected. The following is one of my favorites.

REWARD YOURSELF

One of the best ways to change habits is to reward yourself for your achievements, such as treating yourself to a movie because you skipped a tempting dessert or splurging on a gift because you stopped smoking for a week. Remember that if you use this system, the reward must always **follow** the successful accomplishment of the action. **You cannot give yourself the reward first.** Also, if you do not succeed, you get no reward. And, your reward must follow the success as quickly as possible. When you make pleasure a result of achievement, you tend to want more achievement. The more you succeed in this way, the more you will reinforce the formation of a new habit or the breaking of an old one.

USING SPECIAL ACTIVITIES
AS PERSONAL PAYOFFS

Pick an activity that you do every day, such as watching television. Decide also on an activity that you want to increase, such as exercising or studying. Schedule your activities so that you **must** perform the desired activity before you can do the other. This means you must study before you can watch TV. By doing this, you are using parts of your everyday environment to act on your goals. After several weeks of linking activities together, your autogoal-finder will look for desired behavior every time you think of the reinforcing pleasurable activity. You will have formed a **good** new habit.

RESTRICTIVE ACTION

A man wanted to stop smoking and agreed with his wife that to accomplish this he would do it in steps. First, he made various places in the house taboo areas for smoking, including the dining room, living room and bedroom. This meant that whenever he was in those areas, he could not smoke. As a result he cut down on smoking. He and his wife decided to carry the process one step further and decided he could only smoke alone. Later, he was restricted to smoking only in the corner of his den.

Throughout the process the man knew he could smoke as often as he wanted but only under the self-imposed restrictions. His frequency of smoking was greatly reduced because the restrictions reduced the pleasure of the act. Finally, when he could only smoke in the cellar, he gave up. "I'm not going to go through all that just to smoke," he said. He stopped because the habit was not a comfortable result of the changed environment and action taken. Try this method on habits you want to break. Impose restrictions and see how unattractive the activity becomes.

GIVE YOURSELF POINTS

Sometimes the end result of your habit change program is so far off that you can't feel the reality of your goal. For instance, in a weight loss program the measurement of loss each week is a point system to keep you going, but to discipline yourself to study has no daily or weekly measurement. In such cases, you may want to reward yourself each day in a way that helps you to enjoy immediate benefits, which will reduce the time it takes to get results. Assign points to each hour you spend studying. You could give yourself ten points per hour for each hour spent on subjects you like and twenty points per hour for time spent on those you don't like. Keep a record and add up the points at the end of the week. Now, establish rewards based on what you would enjoy. For example:

> 100 points = A good movie.
> 200 points = Dancing or a night out.
> 300 points = A weekend trip.

Be sure to reward yourself and start the next week with a clean slate and the goal of working toward the coming weekend.

You can do it. You know now how important habit control is to your mind power program. You know that you wear your habits as if they were clothes and that they are obvious to the entire world. You know that you must become aggressive in your approach to others, to your environment and to the way you take action. You realize that you must GEAR up to go up, and developing conscious thought control is necessary to make it all happen. Since you've harnessed your habits, you're ready to use **borrowed mind power.**

POINTS TO REMEMBER

1. Become positively aggressive.
2. Learn to practice **fight** instead of **flight.**
3. Aggressive behavior can quickly become a habit.
4. Use emotion and aggression to reinforce your determination.
5. Develop conscious thought control.
6. Understand what influences your behavior.
7. Remember the EAR formula.
8. Know that you can change your environment either physically or mentally.
9. The results of your actions become the habits that direct your life.
10. Change your world from bad to good and you will change the environment which affects your actions and gives you habit results.
11. Practice habit change techniques by rewarding yourself, by restricting yourself and by putting yourself on a point system.

CHAPTER
10
USE BORROWED MIND POWER

Do you realize how far you've come? You and I have been sharing thoughts that have already helped you gain better control over your life and set you in a new direction toward the things that you want to have and toward becoming the person you want to be.

You've come a long way since the discussion about how special you are and about your fear of moving ahead in or away from your present position. Since then you and I have investigated many of the possibilities that exist in this world. By now you have seen that there are unlimited opportunities for you and many ways you can turn some of those opportunities into wonderful realities. You are beginning to know exactly how your mind works and to realize that your goal-finder is always working as long as you set it in motion. By now you will have had many circumstances in which you've been able to set your goal-finder in motion and stimulate your autogoal-finder to carry you toward victories. In this way, you've been able to program your mind so that as you put in good, powerful information, you reap a harvest of the same.

You know that failure can only come when you quit trying. For that reason you will never give up again. In fact, failure means that you are more experienced than before you failed. Each time you fail, just like Thomas Edison, you find a way that will not work. Your successes live on. Your failures merely end a project, give you experience and free you to go on to the next adventure. Your successes, on the other hand, make you a more competent individual. This competence helps to build your confidence, and your confidence increases your competence, and the competence builds more confidence—on and on.

You have also been cautioned. You realize now that your habits can control you. This can be put to good use or can be a devastating part of your mind power program. Since your habits run you, it is absolutely essential that you harness them.

Harnessing habits means that it is necessary for you to change your behavior. If you change the way you react to situations, you will begin to change your attitudes about circumstances. With this attitude change you will begin to react differently each time and will form new habits. The new habits will increase your ability to become a new person under your mind power to success program.

You have come a long way toward using your own mind power. Now you must also use the mind power of other people. I gave you some examples from my life where it was necessary to support my activities with the help of other people. I also pointed out that I once had and still have many shortcomings. For that reason, I asked for the help of other people who had special talents and abilities that would make up for the shortcomings in my own life. I still do this in a much greater way. Today I enlist the aid of other people on a larger scale. **I constantly use borrowed mind power.**

As you continue in your mind power to success program, you'll find that further progress is virtually impossible without drawing other people into your personal development. You must borrow mind power and form your **brain trust.**

YOU MUST DEVELOP MENTAL HARMONY

Borrowing mind power means more than just receiving ideas from another person. It also means achieving mental harmony with one or many so that the cooperative effort generates more power than anyone had by himself.

As you form a brain trust with someone else, you're actually setting up a system whereby you can obtain the full benefit of that other individual's experience, education and intelligence as if his mind were yours. As a result of tapping that individual's mind, the two of you come together in a harmonious way for the purpose of achieving a specific objective. In doing so, you define your purpose while stimulating and inspiring each other from this mind power harmony. When two people get together under these circumstances, they do so with a feeling of faith that they are going to accomplish whatever goal they have set for themselves. You've already experienced this type of mental power—recall special relationships you've had with friends or with someone you love.

Your goal-finder not only receives information, it also sends information to other individuals. This is done through the actions that result from forming new habits; it is done because as you change into a new individual your entire being becomes a broadcasting station for the "new you" as your image is impressed upon the world. As you set about changing the world around you by using mind power techniques, you will change. Other people will notice the change. You will broadcast your new personality and people will begin to act based on the changes that have taken place in your life. You will energize others to act the way you expect them to and to relate to the new individual you are becoming. The thought seeds that you planted in your mind suddenly have not only produced a harvest within you, but will also have produced a harvest in the minds of others around you. This is not unusual and will happen more frequently as you continue in your mind power to success program. For this reason, you will find it easier to build with another or several a bona fide brain trust in which your minds are in harmony and you all receive the benefit of several minds working together.

BORROWED MIND POWER
STIMULATES THE SUBCONSCIOUS

There is another benefit to working with the mind of one or several individuals when you are seeking a goal. You know that the subconscious mind must be stimulated before you do things well. When you discuss your ideas with others and get them involved as part of your brain trust, they will help stimulate your subconscious mind, as you will theirs, and all the power that resides within the subconscious individually and collectively will be available for your use. This is how borrowed mind power becomes a multiplier of all of the mind power in each individual. When stimulated, the subconscious pours forth information that none of you would have thought of before your discussions.

You've heard of the marvelous ideas that result from two or three people working together. The stimulation of the subconscious causes some of the marvelous results that come from this brain trust method. I told you about Thomas Edison and how he persisted to develop the light bulb. Edison learned how to use the brain trust and knew how to employ other people's mind power. Though Edison lacked a formal education, he still became a great inventor. He borrowed mind power from friends in the scientific world and, of course, from books and articles.

There are two types of situations for which you will use borrowed mind power and form a brain trust:

1. Personal or social reasons, such as the special brain trust relationship that develops between spouses.
2. Professional advancement or business reasons with a personal objective in mind.

If this special brain trust relationship does not exist between you and your spouse, you will have difficulty using borrowed mind power. The harmonious relationships in your life must begin where you live. This also means that for the brain trust developed with your mate to be long lasting and successful, it must be based on the purest of motives—love. The mind power relationship developed on this basis tends to not only coordinate the minds of the individuals, but to also combine the spiritual qualities of the two people involved. The combination of the minds and spirits of the two individuals results in a very powerful force.

I once heard Robert Schuller, the West Coast television preacher, say on his "Hour of Power" program that what we really want out of life is **joy.** Beyond that, he said, we want happiness and the fundamentals of a successful life. As I thought about the relationship which develops from the brain trust between a man and a woman, I decided that it meant exactly what Dr. Schuller was talking about— joy, happiness and the qualities needed for success. **Make sure that the people at the center of your life are at the center of your existence!** This means the people who live with you **physically** must be with you **mentally.** You cannot effectively use borrowed mind power unless this condition exists at the core of your life.

Once you have established this harmonious relationship close to home, you can use the same techniques in your business or career. Think about every successful industry in America and you'll realize that that industry or company was successful due to continued application of the brain trust principles. The managers of that company or particular industry freely use borrowed mind power to achieve daily successes to keep their organization going. Our free

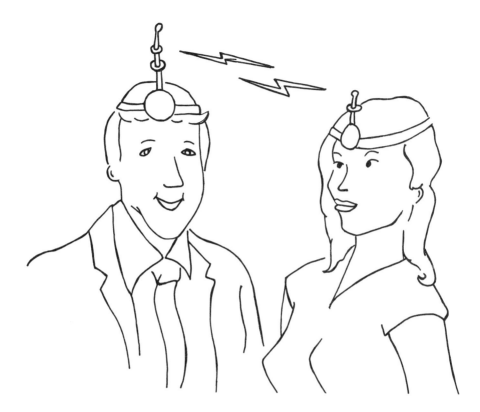

MAKE SURE THAT THE PEOPLE AT
THE CENTER OF YOUR LIFE ARE
WITH YOU MENTALLY.

enterprise society is a tremendous illustration of all of the marvelous economic power that results from the harmony of brain trusts working together toward common objectives. This country became great and remains great because of the freedom of people to get together, stimulate their subconscious minds and become stronger, collectively, than they would be as single contributors to society. People who become rich and powerful do so first by using their personal mind power and second by borrowing mind power from others so that they can achieve their goals.

What I'm saying about borrowed mind power has been proved to be true over and over. A marvelous aspect of mind power is that it is neither the property of large companies nor the secret of any government. Borrowed mind power as used by these companies and governments is also available to you and me. The poorest person on earth can use borrowed mind power to become wealthy. It's simply a matter of choosing to use it. For that reason, as you continue reading this chapter, I'm going to ask you to go beyond the goals that you've established at this point. I want you to imagine other people helping you achieve those goals and then try to see the next logical step beyond achieving your goal. I want you to imagine that your goal has taken you from an average life to one of greatness. Don't put the book down; remember, you have just as good an opportunity to achieve greatness as any other individual. You must aim for high goals when you're using the minds of others in your brain trust. When you use borrowed mind power you must have such exciting goals that they stimulate the imagination and, therefore, the subconscious mind of others.

Memorize the following poem and think about it as you set goals beyond those you set in the first few chapters of this book:

Bargain for Life

I bargained with life for a penny,
And life would pay no more,
However I begged at evening
When I counted my scanty store.

For life is a just employer,
He gives you what you ask,
But once you have set the wages,
Why, you must bear the task.

I worked for a menial's hire,
Only to learn, dismayed,
That any wage I had asked of life,
Life would have willingly paid.

People who are successful in life **never** bargain with life for poverty. In Chapter 9, I said that poverty exists because of generations of poverty thinking. Successful people bargain for the highest wage and life pays it. The successful person you are becoming knows there is power in life that belongs to you as payment for your contribution.

THE SUBJECT OF WAGES

What about the wages you earn for the work you do in your job in society? It all has to do with sowing and reaping.

The other day I spent eight hours talking to a group of salespeople who formed one of the most unmotivated groups I've ever had to turn around. I'm not finished with them yet. They have just begun to learn the concept of giving their employer more than merely adequate work. I shocked several of them when I asked, "How many of you feel you are underpaid?" Many laughed while several gleefully told me the facts of life. When they were finished I told them how pleased I was that they were underpaid.

I said that I've always made sure when I turned in my work to my employer that I was underpaid. I told them that in any situation an employee must give his company 100 percent of what he is paid for **and then some.** They sat stunned and silent. I waited for someone to speak. "What do you mean, Bill?" someone asked.

I said that if our companies don't get more than they pay for, they will not be able to take their investment in their employees and get a suitable return; they need a profit from their laborers in order to grow. If an employer cannot grow, how can the employees? Where will there be room for advancement? How will the company expand? How will anyone be promoted? Furthermore, when I know I've given my company 100 percent of what I've been paid for and then some, I can go home with a clear conscience and feel wonderful about myself. When I feel good about myself everything else in my life is bright. Beyond this, I know that my superiors are going to recognize it and I will eventually reap the harvest. Even if my immediate superior fails to see my extra effort I know that life will reward me. I've found that the more I do the greater the experience I gain. This experience expands my subconscious mind, and the expanded mind never returns to its former shape. Even if I leave my company, I'll take with me all of the experience gained through my extra efforts. As I give more than I receive, I grow at an accelerated pace.

I'm appealing to everyone who believes that there must be an easy way to get more. If you want to get more things out of life, then it's time for you to become wiser than you've ever been before. To do this you must not only borrow mind power from other people, but you must also start now to allow them to borrow your mind power.

There is power for you in giving away or lending the mind power that exists within your brain. That means you have to go beyond what is expected of you in your life, in your job or your business. It's called "going the extra mile."

One of the companies I worked for hired a young man whose position was low man on the totem pole. But when everybody else rushed out of the office at the stroke of five o'clock, John stayed behind for a few moments. I went by his desk one day and asked him if he had lost track of the time. He said, "No, I just wanted to avoid the rush. Besides, there are a few more things I can finish in these quiet moments. By the way, Mr. Stiles, is there anything I could do for you before I go home?" That's going the extra mile.

John did not report directly to me and I really had no extra work. I knew several other executives, however, who were able to use John's services when he asked if he could do more for them. One day while I was talking with the executive vice-president of the company, John poked his head in the room and asked if there was anything he could do. The vice-president said, "Yes, why don't you take this home and read it. Let me know what you think about it in the morning."

The next day John reported on a marketing plan and gave suggestions for how he thought it could be improved. The improvements were those the executive vice-president had already decided to implement, but John had shown that he, too, could think on the executive level. Eventually, John became an executive, rising above many people who had been in the company for ten or twelve years. While others were running home at five, John was going the extra mile. He was giving 100 percent and then some. Now John is able to borrow others' mind power as he directs a division of that company.

Your destiny is in your hands. You have a privilege that is not extended to citizens of other countries—the personal initiative to go the extra mile wherever you are in your life.

I've studied many great men in history and have tried to analyze what made them successful. Every one of the people I analyzed achieved their success by doing more than they were paid for. They went beyond what was expected of them. They allowed their mind power to be borrowed.

Do you have any doubts about what I am saying? If you do, there's only one way to prove or disprove the system of giving more than you get. That is for you to put it to work as part of your daily habits. As you

JOHN USED THE SECRET OF RAISING
HIMSELF FROM CLERK TO EXECUTIVE —
WORKING FOR HIS WAGE
AND THEN SOME.

begin forming the new habits discussed in chapters 9 and 10, I'm asking you to form the habit of giving more than you take in your job. There are some things that cannot be believed until they are proved to you through experiences.

THE BORROWED MIND POWER OF EDUCATION

Look at what happened in America in 1982 and 1983. Look at the steel workers who were out of jobs, at all of the wasted man- and womanpower as the unemployed sat around while changes occurred. What happened? Why were these people unable to adjust to the new world that developed to the right and left of them?

When this country was involved in the deepest part of the recent recession, I made more money than I'd ever made in my life. I quit a steady executive job with a large company and risked going into my own business. As a result, I achieved more than I'd ever had up to that point. How is this possible? The difference between people such as I who prospered during those bleak times and the people who found themselves without work can be summed up in the concept of the borrowed mind power of education.

You must continually educate yourself. You must borrow the mind power of people who have put their experiences in books. You must always be a student and learn from every source around you. You must obtain specialized information which you can use to meet your particular goals. Where can you get this information?

Remember the list of books in Chapter 6? Did you go to your library? Have you begun reading the books? When will you start? The type of education and borrowed mind power I am talking about is absolutely free. Books from your public library cost nothing to borrow and read. Between their covers there is knowledge on nearly every subject imaginable. You have access to thoughts from the beginning of recorded history and can use this knowledge to your benefit. If you have a specific goal in mind, reading all of the information in the library about the subject can stimulate your subconscious and put your goal-finder in action.

YOU CAN GET BORROWED MIND POWER
FROM BOOKS, TAPES, COMPUTERS,
TELEVISION, VIDEO DISCS —
ANY INFORMATION SOURCE.

How did I learn all of the information contained in this book? Very little of it is original. Of course, my experiences are mine, but I can't help feeling that these experiences are merely repetitions of what has happened to people before me. I learned to formulate new ideas by going over the ideas that past masters of thought had long before me. At an early age I developed a habit of going to the public library in both Ellwood City and New Castle to borrow the mind power of men and women who lived many years before I was born. Much of the information in this book regarding psychology, human development and goal-setting aspects of the mind power to success program came from my early study. However, I wasn't ready to write about it then. I still had to take that information and apply it to my own life to make sure that it would work for me as it did for those in the past. Only after having personal proof am I able to give testimony to you and encourage you to go out and do the same.

Because you are reading this book, I know that your program to success—your mind power program—is on its way. Remember, though, your program must be very carefully selected just as you select good food for your diet. If you eat unhealthful food, your body will not respond properly. If your mental meals are not healthful, you cannot expect to grow in your mind power program. To read whatever you get your hands on might be pleasant, but since you have only a limited amount of time, I am going to suggest that your reading be highly selective. As you borrow mind power from authors you must read for a source of education that will help you achieve your goals. Reading comics or sex magazines will not speed you toward any wonderful achievement.

In addition to reading, from this point be sure that your other exposures also are carefully selected to help you achieve what you are trying to do. Recently, I wanted to accelerate my consulting business. Kathy and I decided to go to a professional whom we knew was bringing in more than a million dollars a year through his consulting business. One month after I met with this individual in Washington, D.C., Kathy and I put in motion the ideas and principles that he told us will help our business grow to possibly the same level as his. I went after specialized information to help me quickly achieve what we wanted to do. Was this information given freely? Of course not. We made an investment, but it's one from which we expect to get a return.

I have always realized that if I invest a dollar in the bank I can expect a reasonable return based on the going rate of interest. I've also realized for a long time that if I invested that same dollar in my mind, my return could be ten thousand times the original. I hope that throughout this book I have given you effective examples of how this has happened over and over for me. You must find ways to invest in your mind. Go after the information you need, borrow or buy mind power from other people.

CULTIVATE THE MIND POWER OF FRIENDS

You can't go through life and achieve success without cultivating friends. In business circles friends who are helpful are called "contacts." This is a good word when used the right way. It means that you've established a relationship with someone you can help or who can help you when the occasion arises.

About eight years ago I made a contact with a man in Oklahoma City. We discussed my intention of becoming a motivator of people. He had an opportunity for me to participate in one of his sales meetings with his regional sales managers. I shared with them my ideas about the development of salespeople. My friend sat in on the meeting and later said it was one of the finest sessions that he'd ever had in his company. He told me that if I ever decided to form my own company in the area of training, I should contact him because he wished to be a client. Eight years after that first meeting I did form my own company. My friend in Oklahoma became my first client and a testimonial to others who later added their names to the list of people who needed the same type of sales and marketing training.

You must establish contacts through every possible way. Of course, you want to be careful to make sure that the contacts are those who will help you and not detract.

One of the best ways to establish contacts is through your church. In Chapter 1, I mentioned a friend I had met through church, Bernie McCardle. Bernie is the one who introduced me to Dick Chaput who, in turn, set my thinking in a new direction. The church atmosphere brings people together under very special circumstances where people are inspired to search the spiritual sides of themselves.

No matter where you find them, your contacts are necessary for your growth and well-being. The person who feels that he or she can go it alone is the one who becomes shut inside a shell, turns into an introvert and soon becomes selfish and narrow. This type of person will never be able to take full advantage of his or her mind power because he or she will never be able to form a brain trust.

CHANCES FOR BORROWING MIND POWER SURROUND YOU

Everything in life gives you a chance to borrow mind power. Living itself is a matter of attending a great and wonderful school. Everything that you see or hear or touch in life can inspire thought. Therefore, all of your experiences become teachers. Wise people throughout the ages have included daily life in their educational experience as they contact other minds and come in contact with other objects in this world. By paying attention to people and objects, you can develop your mind as you exchange thoughts and experiences.

The brain trust or borrowed mind power approach really is an unlimited way for you to experience mental growth. It's a way for you to add to the power of your mind with the knowledge, experience and mental attitude of all of the great minds of history as well as the great minds of today.

Think of it this way: If I give you one of my dollars in return for one of yours, each of us will have no more than he started with. But if I give you a thought in return for one of yours, each of us will have gained a 100 percent dividend on his investment of time. A thought is valuable because you can share it with someone and not lose a bit of it yourself. Conversely, another individual can share a thought with you and still retain it. This is probably one of the best ways that I can explain borrowed mind power and the effect it will have on your life. There can be no greater relationship as profitable as two people exchanging their thoughts.

Remember the story in Chapter 3 about the acres of diamonds? The story was a single thought, wasn't it? It told you that you can find riches in your own backyard if you merely look for them. The author of that story, Russell Conwell, was a preacher who got the idea for the story from a janitor in his church. The idea also led to his achieving his goal in life.

Conwell's goal was to establish a college for people who could not afford an education. However, he needed more than a million dollars to get his college started. Conwell was talking to the janitor while the janitor was cutting the church lawn. Conwell mentioned to him that it looked as though the grass on the property next to the church was greener than his own grass. The janitor smiled and said, "Yes, it does look greener over there, but that's because we're too familiar with the grass on our own side of the fence."

There was nothing outstanding about the janitor's comment; however, Conwell's mind had had a seed planted in it which began to produce a harvest. From the janitor's remark, Conwell wrote the story about the diamond mine and called it "Acres of Diamonds." He told that story all over America and earned more than $6 million. When the story was published in book form, it became a best-seller and is still being sold today. (This is one of the books I recommended that you pick up at your library.)

Anyone can help you with your borrowed mind power program. Listen to people. As I travel across the country and lecture to sales people from north, south, east and west, I always pause in my seminars for feedback. I've learned enough over the years to supply me with five full-day seminars. My students have taught me as much as I have taught them. Anyone can help you. Every brain is a possible source of information and inspiration for you. Every brain can give you a thought seed. Some of these thought seeds can be of great value as they help you solve your problems or achieve your goals.

MEXICAN FOOD LED TO
HALF A MILLION DOLLARS IN PROPERTY

While working for a manufacturing company, I was sent to Houston, Texas, to attend a convention. I met a customer of our company, Stuart Garrell from Albany, New York. Stuart and I decided to have a bit of Mexican food the first evening of the convention. During the conversation over dinner, I mentioned that I wanted to do more with my life than merely work for a wage. He asked me why I didn't investigate the possibilities of real estate. We spent the next two hours discussing how I could acquire property. I went home after the convention and talked to my banker about using the equity in my farm to buy that first property. From that point on, I continued to use equity and to pyramid one property after the other until I owned half a million dollars in real estate. That real estate today has appreciated another 30 percent and soon will be worth more than a million dollars—the result of a few hours spent with a man who knew how to do it. Did I borrow mind power? You bet I did.

You never know what small incident will influence your life. You don't know what turn life will take in the future. My conversation with Stuart Garrell involved me in the acquisition of property. As I became further involved in that acquisition, I bought a beauty shop and met Kathy.

You and I, individually, are not smart enough to totally influence all of our steps as we head toward the future. We actually need cooperation from those people who will lend us their mind power. Make sure you understand this. This single thought can help you open many doors to success, can elevate you to high money brackets and can help you toward great individual achievements. To achieve this you must continually seek the company of people who know more than you do. For you to rise above your present level, you must be in the company of people who are your superiors. In this way, you begin to emulate the activity of your chosen associates. If those associates are superior to you, then you will become superior in the future.

HENRY FORD'S DAY IN COURT

Henry Ford sued the *Chicago Tribune* during World War II because of published statements implying that he was an ignoramus. When the case came to court, the lawyers for the newspaper decided to prove that the statements were factual by showing that Ford was really an ignorant individual. They put him on the stand and cross-examined him on many subjects. One of the questions they asked him was, "How many British soldiers were sent to the United States to defeat the colonists in 1776?"

Ford calmly replied, "I don't know just how many, but I've heard that it was a lot more than ever went back." Naturally, the people in the courtroom, including the jury, laughed at this comment.

The questions went on for several hours while Ford answered as best he could, remaining calm throughout the process. He finally got tired of the silly inquisition, and after a question that was particularly stupid, he pointed his finger at the newspaper's lawyer and said, "If I

HENRY FORD PROVED THAT TRUE EDUCATION AND PROPER USE OF THE MIND MEANT CREATIVE THINKING, NOT JUST THE GATHERING OF FACTS AND COLLECTING MISCELLANEOUS TIDBITS OF INFORMATION.

should really wish to answer the foolish question you have just asked, or any of the others you have been asking, let me remind you that I have a row of electric buttons above my desk and by placing my finger on the right button, I can call in men who could get me the correct answers to all the questions you have asked and to many that you have not the intelligence either to ask or to answer. Now, will you kindly tell me why I should bother filling my head with a lot of useless details in order to answer every fool question that anyone may ask when I have able men around me who can supply me with the facts I want when I call for them?''

After he said this, the courtroom was silent. Henry Ford had given an answer that revealed that true education means using the mind, not just gathering facts and miscellaneous tidbits of information. Ford probably could not have worked in his laboratories to produce items needed for his automobiles, but he knew how to use the mind power of other individuals to do these things for him.

When you can use your intellect to pull together the knowledge of other people, you are, like Henry Ford, truly using borrowed mind power for success.

ON TO ACTUAL PRACTICE

In this chapter I've been trying to convince you that it's necessary to draw on other people in the world around you. Further, I am suggesting that you use the objects of education so that you might draw on the mind power of people who have been on the earth before. That means that you want to buy and borrow books and tapes and acquire information from others who can help you shortcut your way to success.

You'll want to start practicing using borrowed mind power with those who are closest to you. Remember, without developing a harmonious relationship with those people at your center of existence you will find it virtually impossible to carry this principle beyond your home environment.

By now, you are well beyond the halfway mark in your mind power to success program. In fact, you have already absorbed most of the principles necessary for you to achieve your objectives. As you get closer to the conclusion of this book and a new beginning in your life, you will have to consider another area that directly affects your mind power, one which can accelerate or destroy your program—the power of enthusiasm.

PUT IT ALL TOGETHER BY SURROUNDING YOURSELF WITH GOOD INFORMATION SOURCES.

POINTS TO REMEMBER

1. For further progress in your mind power to success program, you must form a brain trust with people around you.
2. Set up a system for obtaining full benefit of another individual's experience, education and intelligence.
3. Your goal-finder receives and sends information.
4. Borrowed mind power stimulates the subconscious mind.
5. The brain trust method enables a group to come up with greater ideas than an individual could.
6. Form a brain trust for personal and business reasons.
7. You can't have harmony with the world unless you first have harmony with your mate.
8. People who become rich and powerful do so by using their own mind power as well as borrowing mind power to achieve their goals.
9. Successful people never bargain with life for poverty.
10. Continually educate yourself using borrowed mind power from people who've written books along with tools such as tapes and computers.
11. Chances for borrowing mind power surround you.
12. Remember the thought from "Acres of Diamonds": Opportunity exists in your own backyard.

CHAPTER
11
USE THE POWER OF ENTHUSIASM

You can energize your mind power program, make progress and move quickly toward the happiness of success by injecting one necessary element: **enthusiasm**.

Think of enthusiasm as being similar to the electrical power in the battery of your automobile. The automobile is ready to go. It is mechanically sound, there's gas in the tank and you're ready to begin an important trip. You turn the key to start the engine, but nothing happens. The battery is dead. The electricity necessary to start it is absent. Likewise, without enthusiasm you're not going to get started. Also, once your car is running, it won't continue to function without electricity. That means that your car's generator must provide a constant source of energy. Your own "enthusiasm generator" must do the same thing. For your mind power program to work, **you must harness the power of enthusiasm**.

This is not a short-term project. To harness enthusiasm you must constantly practice being enthusiastic. You must find reasons to be enthusiastic about your daily activities. You must wake up in the morning in a special way and go to bed at night physically and mentally exhausted as a result of your enthusiastic participation in life. In some ways, it's a matter of approaching life in a childlike manner. A child finds the world wonderful; he exhibits enthusiasm for everything he sees and hears. Every day is a marvelous experience. This is how you have to act in order to regain the energy of enthusiasm that you knew as a child.

THINK OF ENTHUSIASM AS BEING SIMILAR TO THE ELECTRICAL POWER IN THE BATTERY OF YOUR AUTOMOBILE.

START EACH DAY WITH AN AFFIRMATION OF ENTHUSIASM

The way you handle the first five minutes of every day will determine the nature of the hours that follow. Many people get up in the morning depressed and asking, "I wonder what is going to go wrong for me today?" Consequently, something does. These people allow the day to happen to them rather than controlling it as a precious gift that can be used to great advantage on the way to success and happiness. The American writer, Henry David Thoreau, spent the first five minutes of every day in bed telling himself about the wonderful opportunities that awaited him. He would think of the activities he was going to be involved with, then would imagine himself enthusiastically participating. In this way, when he finally arose, he was already happily involved in living. This type of early morning mental conditioning will infuse you with a zest for life even before your feet hit the floor.

The moment your feet hit the floor, you'll want to do and say something enthusiastically. You have already conditioned yourself mentally for good, positive activity. Next you'll want to put that thought into action. If your partner in life gets up with you, say something enthusiastic to that person. Sing as you shower. Compliment yourself on your good looks as you gaze into the mirror. Talk to yourself; tell yourself what you're going to do and how much you're going to enjoy doing it. All of this will take no more time than it usually takes you to get ready. The only difference is that while you groom yourself physically, you also groom yourself mentally. Your mental attitude will take on the same good appearance as your physical self. Both, of course, are extremely important. Your physical grooming has been important enough for you to pay attention to it every day, and daily mental grooming is the first step toward harnessing the power of enthusiasm.

START EACH DAY WITH AN
AFFIRMATION OF ENTHUSIASM.

William James, the father of modern psychology, told us that if we want to **be** enthusiastic, we must **act** enthusiastically. This means that you must truly believe in the power of enthusiasm and find topics and projects about which you can sincerely be enthusiastic. To merely act enthusiastically when there is no solid basis for such action would result in failing to harness the power. You would condition yourself toward disbelief in the principle and work into a nonproductive life. To be genuinely enthusiastic you must believe in whatever you choose. The point here is that often your enthusiasm has been secret, hidden so far away that it died. Acting out enthusiasm reinforces the subconscious mind. You know how important programming the subconscious mind is to your mind power program. Once the subconscious is exposed to repeated enthusiasm sessions, it responds and gives a harvest of the same. Enthusiasm will grow in the individual who practices it, who acts enthusiastically about a project in which he firmly believes. This means enthusiasm will become a big part of your life when you start using it from the moment you awaken.

"BILL, HOW DO YOU STAY SO ENTHUSIASTIC?"

During the last hour of an eight-hour seminar one of the attendees asked me how I stayed so enthusiastic after speaking all day. Until that point, I'd never really given it much thought, but what I told that person is still true for me today. I said to the person, "I found a need that other people had and my life involves satisfying that need. I can get truly excited about that and know I can stay excited for the rest of my life." Of course, I was referring to the seminars, books and audio tapes that I produce. At that time, I didn't expand my answer, but after thinking about it, I know that enthusiasm in many people's lives comes from such activities.

If you want to be enthusiastic about what you do, you must feel that you are fulfilling a need in this world. It must be a need that relates to other people and one for which you are ideally suited. Think about the last time that you were extremely helpful to another individual. How did you feel? That's how living an enthusiastic life feels all the time.

Am I suggesting that your work should fulfill another's need? Am I suggesting that you get involved in activities that benefit other people? Am I encouraging you to make sure that your daily activity is productive and makes a worthwhile contribution to society? Absolutely! You cannot live an enthusiastic existence or be energized by the power of enthusiasm unless you are making a worthwhile contribution. You must be able to see the needs of the world and, in your own way, take care of those needs. Individuals who specialize in satisfying needs by using special talents and abilities are the people most sought after in society. They are also the people who obtain financial success and the people you see as the happiest and most fulfilled. They are the group to which you can and must belong. That's why you're reading this book and why you'll want to begin harnessing enthusiasm right now.

Another reason for engaging in productive activities that satisfy a need is so you can believe in yourself, in your value and in the direction in which you are going. Belief in these three areas will make a tremendous amount of difference in the level of enthusiasm you can obtain and maintain every day.

In America today, many workers do not participate enthusiastically in their jobs. Suppose that you are one of them. You work only because you have to earn a living. You merely put in your hours and go home. You're always telling your husband or wife what you don't like about your work. This goes on for some time. Your spouse sympathizes with you and because of mental conditioning, feeds back the same negative information. This reinforces your feelings about your job. The reinforcement solidifies the feeling. Get the picture? This negative activity kills all enthusiasm and results in your spending a major portion of time doing things that you hate. In a mind power to success seminar, I asked a group of workers to find good things in their jobs and think about their activities enthusiastically. They were to try to figure out how their jobs provided for the needs of others. After this mental exercise, they were to go home and talk about the importance of their jobs and how much they enjoyed that particular day. They were to repeat this experiment every other day for one month.

Six weeks later I asked the group if the activity had had any effect. They all reported that the first thing they noticed was how their marriage partner had begun to say nicer things about their company and work. They said that they, too, had begun to enjoy their jobs. Without exception, each individual found that his work had become much easier. Several commented that they expected a promotion within the coming months. Because of an enthusiastic approach they had all gotten their careers back on track and were moving forward at an accelerated rate.

Enthusiastic belief in yourself, your work and your company will make a big difference in your life. If you sow apathy into your job, you will reap apathy. If you say your job is dull, it will be. If, on the other hand, you think of all the wonderful possibilities in your work, you will eventually find new opportunities.

ENTHUSIASM IS SPIRIT FILLED

The first part of the word enthusiasm comes from two Greek words, *en theos,* meaning God within or a spirit within. When we have a spirit for life and living within us, enthusiasm will well out and infect, as well as affect, people around us. There is power in enthusiasm as it is noticed or felt by others. Enthusiasm is catching; it can be transmitted from one individual to another. That's right! If you are around enthusiastic people, you tend to feel their enthusiasm as if you "caught it." When other people are around you, they will feel your enthusiasm, catch it and make it a part of their lives. How about catching some enthusiasm right now?

In addition to the way you start your day and how you think of your job, enthusiasm can be conjured in other ways that will also require commitment. The following suggestions represent powerful how-tos on your way to an enthusiastic approach to life and are keys to help you harness the power of enthusiasm:

1. Convince yourself that you are a very strong person and nothing can shake you. When you do this and repeat the thought over and over each day, you will grow in that direction.
2. Talk about health, happiness and success to everyone, every day.
3. Do the best you can, give your best and look for the best in others.
4. Say something nice to everyone you see.
5. Find something good about all things that happen to you. Think about that good, constantly dwell on it until all negative thoughts are gone.
6. Be happy about the successes of other people. Say over and over why you want others to continue succeeding. Chase away

all feelings of jealousy. Renew your commitment to be success- ful yourself.

7. Never dwell on your mistakes. Put all mistakes behind you and move on to other achievements.
8. Look and be friendly. Smile at everyone you see.
9. Spend so much time on daily self-improvement that you will not have time to criticize others.
10. Become too big to worry, too calm for anger and too self-assured to fear anything. Be so happy that problems will not get you down.

These rules, followed daily, will increase your enthusiasm. You will notice that many of them center around kindness toward other people. As you become more and more involved in your mind power to success program, you will find this to be a very necessary part of your development. When I dwell on this thought, I am reminded of a verse by an anonymous poet that speaks of the kindness we should enthusiastically project to others:

I Shall Not Pass This Way Again

Through this toilsome world, alas!
Once and only once I pass;
If a kindness I may show,
If a good deed I may do,
To a suffering fellowman,
Let me do it while I can.
No delay, for it is plain,
I shall not pass this way again.

What wonderful power there is in the use of enthusiasm for you and everybody around you. Enthusiasm is a state of mind that energizes you to action so that you can accomplish things. It fuels your goal-finder. It's contagious and others will respond. It's power- ful and will help guide your entire mind power program. It's no mere figure of speech; enthusiasm is a vital force that you can harness and use.

Without enthusiasm you are destined to live a life of mediocrity, but with enthusiasm you can achieve greatness. Put yourself in situations that will help advance your enthusiasm program. Try these six steps:

1. Make sure you are working at what you love to do most.

2. Make sure that you are with other people who are also enthusiastic and optimistic.
3. Set your financial goals so that you can feel success often.
4. Take care of your health; be sure you feel good physically.
5. Be sure that you are serving others in some constructive and helpful way.
6. Dress up; when you dress up, you feel up.

As I close this chapter on enthusiasm and as you begin a new chapter in your life, remember that to become enthusiastic you must make enthusiasm a dominant factor in your life. Be alive in a new way. Make sure you possess a contagious enthusiasm that affects everyone around you. Take the advice of the Bible in Eph. 4:23, "Be renewed in the spirit of your mind." When you are renewed in the spirit of the mind, you will be renewed in enthusiasm and can be all that you're meant to be.

POINTS TO REMEMBER

1. Energize your mind power program with enthusiasm.
2. Think of enthusiasm as an electrical power.
3. Start each day with an affirmation of enthusiasm that will infuse you with a zest for life.
4. If you act enthusiastically you will be enthusiastic.
5. If you want to be highly enthusiastic about an activity, find one that fills the needs of others.
6. You must believe in yourself, in your value and in the direction you are going.
7. Remember that enthusiasm is spirit filled and eventually will well up within you and infect others.
8. Remember that you won't pass this way again and you have a choice of living either a life of mediocrity or one infused with enthusiasm.

CHAPTER
12
PRACTICING YOUR MIND POWER

You know you have mind power. Using your wonderful capacity to change opportunity into reality is vitally important. You must get in action and stay in action until you develop a new habit.

This chapter concentrates on several how-to exercises to help you practice using your mind power. After you've practiced, you will be able to transfer your learning exercises to achieve even more than the five goals discussed in this chapter. These goals are those most commonly sought and are objectives that I have achieved. You can select one or several of these goals to practice building your mind power and gain control of whatever controls you.

In this chapter you will not only learn how to practice your mind control, but you will also be introduced to a new concept—developing a mind power trance. The method for getting in touch with your autogoal-finder involves meditation that will put you in a trance and create a mental environment allowing you to program your auto-goal-finder. The five areas for practicing mind power are:

Losing weight.
Giving up smoking.
Overcoming insomnia.
Developing a better memory.
Overcoming shyness.

Achievement of any one of these goals will prove that your mind power system works.

REMEMBER THE NECESSITY OF BELIEF

As you begin, remember: The "how to do it" will work for the person who believes it **can be done!** As you begin the exercises you must believe that you will succeed. You must expect great results. That expectation will be your driving force. Belief is the powerful driving force, the mind power, behind all great achievements. It is the force necessary for every success in church, politics, business and life. Belief that your endeavor will be successful is absolutely essential to your accomplishment!

Don't start the exercises with an attitude of, "Okay, I'll try it, but it probably won't work." That will only give you **negative** power.

If you have any disbelief, you're better off waiting to start these exercises. Remember from previous discussions that your auto-goal-finder is affected by the way you program it. Your mind will develop logic to support your disbelief and your subconscious will work against you. Believe that you won't succeed and you won't. Think success; imagine the feeling of victory. Pretend to be enjoying the results to come and your subconscious will work to make them a reality.

Is this a review? Certainly. But you know that reinforcement is necessary and I want to be sure you are properly prepared for the exercises that are coming.

Remember, you become what you imagine you are.

Look at the person who is a member of the mass of mediocrity. That person actually believes that he has little worth; therefore, he gets less and less from life. He is convinced that he has no importance; therefore, nothing he does is deemed important. As he goes through life, he gets smaller and smaller because he believes less and less in himself and supports this belief by his daily activities. This belief is further supported by nothing coming his way.

Other people always see in you what you see in yourself; therefore, others will reinforce the "shrinking man" who is diminishing daily in the eyes of those around him. This depressing situation is the result of disbelief.

What about the "up" side? The "up" side is **you,** the person who is moving ahead, improving, using mind power to success. You are one who **believes!** You know that you're worth all that life can give you; you're ready to ask for more. You know that your contributions are valuable because you are worthwhile. Since you know you are worth much, you will receive much. Go for it!

REMEMBER, YOU ARE WHAT
YOU IMAGINE YOU ARE.

BECOMING MORE BY WEIGHING LESS

The first goal on the list is one that is set by millions of people every day: losing weight. Many people want to lose weight so that they can be what they imagine they should be. This is sufficient reason for making this an objective of your mind power program. Weigh less to become more in your mind's eye. But if weight loss is not your objective, don't stop reading. Also in this segment is the technique of mind power trance, something required to achieve all five goals.

To accomplish your mind power objectives, you must be able to push your own buttons. To do that you must be in touch with your goal-finder through programming. When you program your goal-finder, you are contacting your subconscious mind and telling it how you want your behavior to be changed. To do this, you must achieve a special mental state. You must induce a mental fixation that is actually a mind power trance.

To induce or achieve the proper mind power trance, select a private place where you will not be disturbed. Make sure there is no telephone and little possibility of noise or interruption. Lower the lights and, if it helps you to relax, play soft music with a slow beat. Experiment to create an environment that is so pleasant you feel you want to sleep.

Relax. Lie down or recline in a comfortable chair and raise your feet. Be sure your clothes are loose and comfortable and that you have no appointments or other time pressures. Breathe deeply and slowly, then close your eyes while you tell yourself that you're going to relax every muscle in your body. Concentrate on relaxing your feet first then progressing all the way to your face. This is a toe to head relaxation exercise. Remind yourself that physical relaxation is always mind controlled and is the first success for you as you achieve a mind power trance.

YOU MUST INDUCE A MIND POWER TRANCE TO GET IN TOUCH WITH YOUR SUBCONSCIOUS.

Once you have achieved a relaxed, receptive mood, you will be in your mind power trance and ready to program your autogoal-finder through suggestion. Just as you are subject to being programmed through the suggestions of other people you are also subject to being programmed by your own thoughts. As you practice this auto-suggestion, you will increase your ability to program your goal-finder and gain greater use of your mind power. This is very much like hypnotism, or hypnotic autosuggestion. It's worked for centuries and will work for you now.

At this point, you must check to be sure you have achieved a mind power trance by using the eye closing test and the swallowing test.

For the eye closing test, focus on an item in the room. Be sure it is at a distance and in a shadow so that you have to strain slightly to see it. You want to get your eyelids to close at the count of ten. As you count, tell yourself that your eyes are getting heavy, you are tired and want to close them. When you experience the irresistible urge to close your eyes, you will know that you have reached a state where your subconscious mind is open to your conscious suggestions. You have achieved a mind power trance.

If you don't succeed at first, count to ten again. You were probably not relaxed and need further suggestion. Eventually, you will be successful. Here is a suggestion of what you can say to achieve your mind power trance:

I am now counting to ten as I focus on the object. As I count to ten, my eyelids will become extremely heavy and I will become very, very tired. Before I finish the count of ten, I will want to close my eyes. The strain of looking at that object will become increasingly stronger and the urge to rest will also become irresistible. I will always be awake, able to hear everything and make suggestions to my subconscious:

1. I am becoming very, very tired.
2. My eyelids are very heavy and want to close.
3. My eyes are straining and becoming watery.
4. I can barely keep my eyes open; I must close them to relieve the strain.
5. My eyes are starting to close.
6. My eyes are closing more and more; I am beginning to feel more and more relaxed.

7. My eyes feel better when they are closed.
8. My eyes are closed and it is impossible for me to open them at this point.
9. I have achieved a mind power trance.
10. My subconscious mind will listen to my conscious control and do whatever I tell it.

When you find your eyes closing automatically, you are ready to program the subconscious.

Next, try the swallowing test. Say to yourself:

This time as I count to ten, I will find that I must swallow. I will not be able to overcome the urge to swallow. Before I count to ten, I must swallow. I will not feel normal until I swallow. The urge to swallow will stay with me until I satisfy it:

1. My lips are very, very dry.
2. I am very thirsty and must swallow.
3. The urge to swallow is becoming overwhelming and I find it hard to resist.
4. I can resist no longer.
5. I am so thirsty I must swallow now.
6. I am going to swallow.
7. I cannot stop from swallowing.
8. The urge is strongest now.
9. I must swallow now.
10. I have swallowed once which means that I have achieved a mind power trance. I can tell my subconscious mind what I want it to do. I am in touch with my autogoal-finder and will put it into action.

While doing this test be sure you swallow without voluntary action. You must repeat the test until this happens. When it happens, you are in touch with your subconscious mind and can give it the suggestion you want it to follow. You are using your total mind power.

Be sure before you start inducing your mind power trance that you've planned to tell your subconscious what you want your auto-goal-finder to achieve for you. In this way, you will be able to program for results.

Now, on with losing weight through mind power. There are seven basic steps that should be dealt with one at a time per mind power session:

1. **Make a definite decision.** During your first mind power trance session, tell yourself that you are deciding to do something about being overweight. Make sure that you are in a trance before you tell your subconscious mind that this decision is final and unchangeable. Admit that you have a problem and are going to do something about it.

2. **Give your subconscious reasons for your losing weight.** Before this second session, write down all of the reasons for you to lose weight. Read medical information that tells how overweight people shorten their lives. Read about illnesses common to overweight people. Remind yourself that insurance rates go up for overweight people because they are considered higher risks than normal weight people. Be ready to put all of this information into your subconscious during your second mind power trance.

3. **Explain why you are losing weight.** You must be motivated to lose weight. You must tell yourself before your third mind power trance why you want to lose weight, then, during your trance, tell your subconscious why losing weight is important to you. Following your session, repeat all the reasons you have for losing weight. This will further strengthen your resolve.

4. **Establish why you are overweight.** Before you go into your fourth mind power trance, figure out why you are overweight. List everything you eat that's wrong for you. Think about the number of times you eat and the size of the portions. Go into your fourth mind power trance and tell the subconscious mind why you are overweight.

5. **Memorize everything you may eat.** In preparation for session five, you must give yourself some good, positive input about the things that you may eat and still lose weight. List everything you may eat based on diet information or your doctor's advice. Memorize these items before going into your mind power trance. You will not be able to read the list while programming your subconscious, so you must move the information from your conscious mind to the subconscious through memory. Once you have achieved your mind power trance, tell yourself over and over what you can eat.

6. **Reinforce your weight reducing goal.** Establish how much weight you are going to lose. Use good medical advice. A rule of

thumb is lose no more than five pounds each month. During this sixth session, tell your subconscious that you will do everything to lose one pound a week, five pounds a month, until you have achieved your goal. You'll begin to see your weight come down and your friends will comment. When this happens, your self-image will improve. All of this will come together as a conscious reinforcement of your program. While you are in your sixth mind power trance, tell yourself the nice things other people have said. This will program your subconscious to seek more compliments and will help you stay on your program so you receive more of these rewards.

7. **Use a daily mind power trance for repetition.** After you've gone through the first six steps, this seventh mind power trance should be repeated every day. The content of this session is a wrap-up of the previous six. Tell yourself that you will follow all of the steps. Tell your subconscious that you can and will stay at your selected weight because you have developed better eating habits and enjoy the comments of your friends. Tell yourself that you are getting healthier every day as a result of your program, that your subconscious is helping you control your life. Tell yourself that when you become consciously weak, your subconscious will help you stick to your program. Tell yourself that your goal-finder sees you at the proper weight and will automatically help you stay there.

This program will work for you. It has worked for me. I maintain my weight at the level I want it. I have never imagined myself as skinny; I keep my weight where I feel it best fits my personality and my self-image. You should decide your weight goal on the same basis. Remember, extremely thin is not the answer. What you believe is right for you is what you should become.

Also, losing weight will improve your appearance and prolong your life. Plus, keeping your weight in check will keep you from developing health problems that usually arise from being overweight, such as hardening of the arteries, heart disease, diabetes and respiratory difficulties. Losing weight will help change your personality by improving your self-image. You will feel proud that you have accomplished a difficult task. You will have increased energy and will be more attractive to the opposite sex. When you've accomplished your weight loss goals, you will feel inspired to conquer other problems, such as smoking. Can you beat that habit?

STOP SMOKING THROUGH
THE MIND POWER TRANCE

Now that you've learned to achieve a mind power trance, you can enforce your behavior modification system and use mind power to stop smoking.

First, educate yourself regarding the smoking habit and establish some facts about what it does to your body. Even though nicotine stimulates the nervous system, it is a poison. Animals have been put to death with concentrated amounts of nicotine. While the amount of nicotine contained in tobacco is not sufficient to kill humans, its cumulative effect is extremely harmful to your health. It's been proved that tobacco smoke destroys lung cells and tobacco causes lung cancer. How do insurance companies look at smoking? Many offer a reduced premium for nonsmokers. Doctors recommend that patients with respiratory problems or heart disease stop smoking immediately. The reason for this is, as it says on a pack of cigarettes, "Smoking is dangerous to your health." But you **can** stop smoking. It's merely a habit and you know that habits can be broken or overcome. This is not a matter of willpower, it's a matter of **mind power**. You must condition yourself to break the smoking habit.

As a former smoker, I can attest that after I quit I slept better, no longer suffered from heartburn and had whiter teeth. Plus, I felt better about myself. What about nervous tension? It has been proved that when tense people chain-smoke, they move to the stage where they become addicted to nicotine the same as they would become addicted to alcohol. Many chain-smokers feel that if they don't have a cigarette, they'll have a nicotine fit. A heavy smoker is rarely relaxed. Yet, I've noticed that chain-smokers usually are not pleased with their habit. In fact, most of them do not enjoy smoking. But they got the habit, then the habit "got" them.

During your mind power trance sessions to break the smoking habit forever tell yourself the following:

1. **You've made a definite decision.**   Tell yourself you will not go back on this decision. It's **now** for the rest of your life. You will stop smoking and never go back to it.
2. **Smoking is dangerous to your health.**   List all of the reasons you want to stop smoking and repeat them daily for at least a week. Tell yourself about health problems such as lung cancer. Think of the horror stories that you've heard. This will give you the motivation necessary to quit.
3. **Smoking can never help you.**   It only tears you apart mentally and physically. Explain to yourself that you want to feel as good as you possibly can and that cigarettes stand in the way of this feeling.
4. **You will not buy any more cigarettes.**   Convince yourself that you will be embarrassed to make the purchase; it indicates that you are weak. You don't want to be weak; therefore, you won't buy any more.
5. **Staying away from cigarettes makes you successful.**   The longer you avoid smoking, the more you can congratulate yourself through your subconscious about the success of your mind power program. Tell yourself that now you'll give up smoking forever. Tell yourself how proud you feel about quitting.
6. **The power of your mind is stronger than your smoking habit.** Tell yourself that since your mind helped you develop the habit, by taking control of your subconscious, you can break it. Remember how cigarettes stink after they've been in an ashtray. Think about how cigarette smoke smells in clothing and hair. Think about tobacco stains on teeth and fingers. Notice how a room smells after people have been smoking. Promise yourself that you'll never be part of that again.

MIND POWER CAN HELP YOU SLEEP

Statistics tell us that more than half of the population of the United States suffers from restlessness or insomnia. That means that more than a billion sleeping pills are sold to Americans every year. For that reason, overcoming insomnia is included as a major objective. My insomnia occurred when I was going through my divorce. My children seemed lost to me and I had many problems in my business and professional life. I found I had to take care of my insomnia without sleeping pills and use, instead, the mind power techniques that I'd already learned.

What is causing your sleeplessness? You could be taking your problems to bed with you or you might just think that you're unable to sleep. It might be that you are sick and suffering some sort of distress or have aches and pains that don't allow you to fall asleep. You might have a mattress that is too hard or there could be a tremendous amount of noise outside your bedroom window. Some people have guilt feelings about many aspects of their lives that keep them from sleeping, or sleeplessness might just be a result of bad habits such as watching late night television instead of turning off the tube and allowing natural sleep to take over.

Whatever the reason, you must analyze your situation and develop the habit of getting the rest you need to revitalize your body and mind for the coming day. You want to be ready to take advantage of all the opportunities that could become realities. Make the following points a part of your mind power trance program to solve your sleeplessness:

1. **Go to bed at the same time every night.** This way, you will establish a pattern that your body will automatically respond to after you have disciplined yourself for twenty-one to thirty days.
2. **Remove obstacles to falling asleep.** If your bed is too hard, get another. If there is a lot of noise, move to a quieter location.
3. **Use your mind power trance techniques to relax.** Start with the muscles in your toes and end with the muscles in your forehead. Do this for at least ten minutes every night, then allow yourself to drift off to sleep.
4. **Sleep for excellence.** Once you've achieved your mind power trance, tell yourself that when you don't sleep, you're not at your best the next day and, therefore, will have more problems to worry about the next night.
5. **Don't say that you can't sleep.** Don't allow yourself to think that you have a persistent problem. Tell yourself sleeplessness is not normal and you're going to change that. Say that you expect to fall asleep soon and continue to tell yourself that until the sleep is real.
6. **Don't move for the first ten minutes in bed.** Let yourself relax. Don't toss or change position; lie very still. This will calm you and reinforce all of the programming you're giving your subconscious mind. Your autogoal-finder will take over and put you into a deep, restful sleep.

7. **Once you're in bed, don't get up.** Don't turn on the lights or read. Don't watch television. Follow your plan as outlined here. Go over the steps repeatedly until you develop a habit of drifting into a comfortable sleep after ten minutes.
8. **Think nice thoughts in bed.** Tell yourself that the problems will wait until tomorrow and think of pleasant situations. You will begin to look forward to these fantasy sessions and the anticipation will make it easier each time to achieve a restful, sleepy state.

When you can't sleep, it could be that something is wrong in your life. By using your mind power trance program, you'll be able to isolate your problems and save them for the daytime. However, you should learn to relax during the day so that you're not uptight at night. This is one of the biggest lessons I had to learn. There is a tendency to carry the worry of the day into the evening and into your bed. Be sure you practice your mind power relaxation exercises every night so that you can continue to reinforce programming your subconscious.

MEMORY IMPROVES THROUGH MIND POWER PROGRAMMING

I took a chemistry course and had a difficult time memorizing the periodic table of elements. This wasn't my only problem. I couldn't assimilate the information the professor was giving. I was halfway through the course and my marks were close to a failing grade. I decided I had to use my knowledge of mind power programming to improve my grade and, consequently, received a high "C" in the class. I used a tape recorder to help me. I put all of my lecture notes on tape and listened to them over and over while in a mind power trance.

I learned that I could assimilate the information more quickly if I put myself into a trance and programmed my subconscious mind. The subconscious set my autogoal-finder in motion to tell me that I would remember everything I heard. After these sessions, I required only one or two exposures to the information before I remembered it.

Tell your subconscious that you are going to improve your memory. Once you have done that, immediately feed the information into your subconscious during your mind power trance. Combine the tape recorder with your mind power trance programming. Put the information on tape and listen to it at least twice. You'll find that your memory will be greatly improved. Once you start to develop the habit of telling your subconscious mind that your memory has improved, it will help you remember ordinary, everyday items.

This seems like a miracle because few people actually use mind power trance programming. Is it new? No, mind power trance programming has been used for centuries. However, society, in its practical, scientific way, has forgotten about the power within the mind and people have stopped using the techniques. There is no need for you to go on without the mind power for a fulfilled life. Even improving your memory makes you a better person in every way, every day.

OVERCOMING SHYNESS THROUGH THE MIND POWER TRANCE

Many people want to change their personalities, particularly those who feel they're too shy to cope with society. This section on overcoming shyness can also help with handling other personality difficulties. The personality you exhibit is really an expression of what is happening inside you. It's the way you communicate the person that you are. The way you dress, the way you walk and talk, the expressions on your face, all of your habits and the way you do things show others who and what you really are. Shyness is a part of you and it indicates that in some cases, you are not sure about how your overall personality fits in with others. To change this, the first thing you have to do is understand what caused the shyness in the first place.

Your first mind power trance session has to be one of analysis. Nobody knows better than you, at least in your subconscious, why you feel shy. At your first session, ask yourself that. You will soon find that your shyness possibly stems from inexperience or uncertainties because you have avoided certain situations. Can you change your personality to reverse the process that makes you shy? Can you feel as if you want to participate in various activities that will broaden your outlook? The answer is "Yes."

It's difficult to change your height. It's also difficult to change other physical parts of you except weight, but many psychologists say that people can change three parts of their personality: habits, traits and attitudes.

You know that a habit is something you do repeatedly. A trait is a little different in that you do it repeatedly, but not the same way each time. An attitude is a way of looking at a part of life. From your attitude you develop a way of conducting yourself; the resulting activity reinforces the attitude and soon the behavior is firmly established.

Traits, habits and attitudes are acquired not inherited situations, and you can do something about them; but first, you must want to change.

You can acquire the personality you want through your mind power trance program. You can change many aspects of your personality once you decide to and have applied the techniques discussed. In fact, many people find that the mind power trance program helps them to develop a personality that attracts other people, and many individuals who have used the techniques started out as shy.

One of the best ways to overcome shyness is to improve your communication talents. When you feel you can communicate with people, you have a tendency to do more of it. Often it means you must improve your vocabulary. When you develop a good vocabulary, you'll become confident in expressing yourself to others. This confidence will make you want to communicate, and shyness begins to disappear after the first exchanges take place in conversation.

Don't get caught up in the idea that a formal education is necessary for a good vocabulary. Anyone can learn words and how to use them properly. You must take the time and energy to look up words that you've heard in conversation whose meanings are not familiar to you. If your vocabulary is limited, your chances of success will also be limited, particularly if you hear words among your friends and associates that you don't understand.

Many people have stagnant minds because they don't know the meanings of enough words to allow their minds to exercise concepts. Consequently, they don't feel confident in social situations and say that they are shy. Words are the tools of thought; you can't think without words. You must express yourself so as to convey thought to another individual.

The words you use and how you use them project your personality. If you're shy, it's probably because you avoid situations where you are required to communicate. Undoubtedly, you avoid those situations because you haven't mastered the English language. With words at your command, you'll have people in command, too.

This is also the time to use the mind power trance program. When you hear an unfamiliar word, find its definition, how it's used and put it on tape. Once you have achieved the mind power trance, use the tape recorder. The words and meanings will go into your subconscious and come out whenever you need them.

SUCCESS THROUGH MIND POWER TRANCE PROGRAMMING

You can lose weight and quit smoking, get more rest, develop a better memory and overcome shyness through mind power trance programming. Is that all you can do? Of course not. You now know principles and techniques that can be applied in any situation: You can master your emotions and overcome depression; you can change unhappy moods into happy ones; you can develop a new personality and achieve control over others; you can even make a success of your marriage if you will search for solutions during your mind power trance.

YOU NOW HAVE IT—GO TO IT!

This book has simply been an explanation of the talents you've always had. These capabilities have resided within you from the moment you were born.

I've always regretted that society does not provide specialized education that allows everyone to maximize individual talents and excel. However, as I write this paragraph, I feel a sense of satisfaction because you and I have shared the knowledge of how you can use your mind power to change all of your opportunities to realities.

You've always had mind power and now you know how to use it—go to it!